King Alfred's
Winchester

Martial Rose Library
Tel: 01962 827306

Check for Disk

1 3 JUN 2008   1 5 DEC 2009

2 3 MAY 2012

- 5 MAY 2009
- 7 MAY 2009
No RENEWA

1 3 MAY 2013

1 7 JUN 2009
1 9 JUN 2009
1 DEC 2009

To be returned on or before the day marked above, subject to recall.

D1610059

KA 03228

ISBN: 978-2-85181-649-8
© 2007 L'Arche *Éditeur*
86, rue Bonaparte, 75006 Paris
Tous droits réservés
contact@arche-editeur.com
Photo de couverture et p. 3 : Jutta Geike et Werner Klammer
© Ursula Kaufmann

La loi du 11 mars 1957 interdit les copies ou reproductions destinées à une utilisation collective. Toute représentation ou reproduction intégrale ou partielle faite par quelque procédé que ce soit sans le consentement de L'Arche est illicite et constitue une contrefaçon ; elle doit donc faire l'objet d'une demande préalable adressée à L'Arche.

Conception graphique : Susanne Gerhards

Kontakthof

with Ladies and Gentlemen over "65"
mit Damen und Herren ab „65"
avec des dames et messieurs au-dessus de « 65 » ans
con signore e signori oltre « 65 » anni

A piece by / Ein Stück von / Une pièce de / Un pezzo di

Pina Bausch

L'Arche
Éditeur à Paris

Kontakthof

with Ladies and Gentlemen over "65"

A piece by PINA BAUSCH

English version by Jo Ann Endicott

Kontakthof is a place where people meet who are searching for contact.
To show yourself, to deny yourself.
With fears. Desire.
Disappointments. Desperation.
First experiences. First attempts.
Tenderness and what arises from,
was an important theme in the work.
Another, for example, was Circus.
Showing part of yourself, overcome oneself.

Kontakthof was performed for the first time 1978 in Wuppertal.
Afterwards in many other countries.
My wish, to see this Piece, this Theme
shown by Ladies and Gentlemen with more Life experience
grew with time even stronger.
So I found the courage, to give *Kontakthof* to elderly people over '65'.
People from Wuppertal.
Neither Actors. Nor Dancers.

In February 2000 we were ready.

At first was planned a one time Happening.
That is why the making of this Film took place so quickly.
Nobody had the slightest idea that *Kontakthof with Ladies and Gentlemen over "65"* would travel to so many different European countries in the following years.

Pina Bausch

Dialogues

First Part

Good evening. I come from Paris!
I come from Hamburg, and I'm married.

*

You're so handsome!
You're so strong!
You're fantastic!

*

He looks like a frog. – Yes, and those...
Fish eyes. – Yes, and sauerkraut hair.
She probably suffers from hair loss.
And I think her skirt could... – Like a tadpole, a frog.
Yes, and that nose! Like cauliflower.
Like two noses in one. – Yes, and those ears...
Look. Now he's touching her.

One, two, three...

The tiny legs and stout body. – And her aggressive femininity.
Wonder if she was that ugly as a child? – I bet she was.
And she has sauerkraut hair, too.

I stand at the end of the piano and threaten to fall.
But before I fall, I scream.
Really loud, so nobody will miss it.
Then I crawl under the piano.
I look out...
...reproachfully.
And I act as if I wanted to be alone.

But in reality, I want someone to come over to me.
Then I take my scarf
and attempt to strangle myself,
in the hope that someone will come
before I die.

*

Hey, I'd like to go for dinner.
Yes, that sounds really good!
I'll invite you.
That's very nice. Where shall we go?
I know a nice place. – What kind of restaurant is it?
Is it here in Wuppertal? – No, it's not in the city.
Italian.
No, I don't feel like Italian at all.
Sure you do. – How about something hearty?
Pork chops with cabbage and mashed potatoes.
Or we could have something else.
They have potato pancakes with bacon and onions?
Yes, but we have to go into town for that. – Yes, maybe
that's better.
I wouldn't mind some potato pancakes. – With sugar and
cinnamon!
Cutlets are delicious, too, with cooked ham.
Cabbage with potatoes and bacon.
And what shall we have for dessert?
Rice pudding with sour cherries.
Ice cream with hot cherries.
Yes. Or waffles! That would be delicious, too.
And some coffee to go with it. A nice cup of coffee.

*

Owww!

*

Where are you?
In the theatre?
Me, too.
We'll see each other in the lobby during intermission.
You're going to come down?
Because of your suit?
That's nonsense.
I'll take a good look at everyone.
I'll recognize you.
There are dancers on stage.
Do you see them?
What did you say?
I shouldn't cry?
Where are you now?

*

Hello, Peter!
Hello, Peter!
Show me what you've learned.
Show me the hip-step that you learned.
Take off your jacket, I can't see anything.
That's supposed to be the step we practiced so long?
Look at me. And right... and centre... and left.
And centre... and right.
Turn around. I want to see that from behind.
Pull your jacket up.
You must be joking.
Turn around and face this way. Look at me.
Big, large circles.
Left, and centre, and right.
Oh, Peter, it's not like that!
Now do it stepping forward.
Oh, Peter, that's not it at all! How long did you...
What did you do while we were rehearsing?
You'll never learn it. You'll need another year!

Andreas, music!

*

One, two, three...

*

Oh, that was lovely! Inge, why don't we try in black?
Yes, in black!
Ready?
Andreas, music!
Enough. No, it's not so good in black, after all.

*

Head!
Cheek!
Chest!
Stomach!
Knee!

*

I'm not angry, I just want to be alone.

Hey, Werner, what's the matter? Are you sick again?

I'm not angry! I just want to be alone.

That would be a change, wouldn't it?
You're worthless and good for nothing!

Ursula!
Ursula!

God, now you're dead, or what?
Probably not even that, you pimply old fart.
Typical. Everyone else is up and you're down.
No pep, no spirit...

A lazy slacker!

What's he up to? –He's going to stink up the air.
Oh, he smokes.

You're a zero, a total loser!
A nitpicky old fart.

What small eyes he has.
His cigarettes are all he needs to see. – People with small
eyes are mean.

A life at your side... But you don't have a side.
You wimp, you bore me!

He looks like a big baby, don't you think?
Yeah, those droopy cheeks. – And look at his stubby fingers...

You're a joke, a spineless creature!
If he buys rolls, he can take his fingers as sausages.
How fidgety he is, squirming around on his chair like that.
The way he chain-smokes,
his life must really be a mess.

Oh, our little wallflower has sneaked her way back.

Look, she's got parsley between her teeth.
He probably doesn't know anyone.

You're a born mistake.

No soap either, huh? – If he had soap, he'd use it on his teeth.

God, how could I get mixed up with you? I must have been
blind.

13

Imagine, she chews parsley and he never washes.
Smells like it, doesn't it? He probably ate a whole bulb of garlic.
And I bet he has no friends if he smells that bad, huh?
And spring onions. – I think it's called *nouvelle cuisine*.
A smelly man is a lonely man, I'm telling you.
Yes, that's how he looks. Look at those socks!
Haven't been washed in weeks.
I think they're made of silk.
Though they smell so good.
He's probably proud of himself, I tell you.

Werner!

I can't stand it anymore. I have to go now, Jutta.
It's just too horrible.

Werner?
Werner?

*

Ich lasse meinen Körper schwarz bepinseln, schwarz bepinseln
Und fahre zu den Fidschi-Inseln, zu den Fidschi-Inseln
Dort ist noch alles paradiesisch neu
Ach, wie ich mich freu, ach, wie ich mich freu
Ich trage nur ein Feigenblatt
Mit Muscheln, Muscheln, Muscheln
Und geh mit einer Fidschi-Puppe
Kuscheln, kuscheln, kuscheln
Aus Bambus richt ich mir 'ne Klitsche ein
Ich bin ein Fidschi, will ein Fidschi sein.

*

…We must have been about twelve or thirteen.
We were always looking for ways to be near the girls.
It wasn't easy at school: girls on the left, boys on the right.

But one day we were allowed to go on an outing,
get out of the city for a day and visit a farm out in the country.
But we were also given a job to do: pick the potato beetles
off the plants.
In those days the girls were...
They wore lovely dresses, pretty blouses and skirts.
As we fanned out over the potato field...
The girls led the way, and we were unobserved for once...
So we said to ourselves, "Let's pass them!"
We started to run, and then it happened:
One of the girls stumbled and fell into a furrow.
She was lying there, with...

Suddenly he took off his shirt. His back was covered with tattoos.
I'd never seen anything like it. Then I turned and ran away.

I was about eighteen years old,
and I had met a man who was about twenty years older.
He was the man of my dreams: dark eyes, black hair...
But, sad to say, I wasn't his dream woman.
He kept telling me, "Child, you're just too young for me."

I still hadn't decided when I got to Döppersberg:
Should I visit
the dark-haired, brown-eyed beauty in Barmen,
or the blonde with blue eyes
and the sweet smile who lived in Vohwinkel?
So I said to myself, "Why not let the cable railway decide?"
"Just get on the next train that comes, and off you go!"
So I hurried and bought
some flowers and got on the next train.

Shall I wear the low-cut, colourful dress,
or better the black, see-through one?
So I looked in the mirror and thought, 'Oh, no!'

There was the pimple that always appeared on the middle of my forehead
when I had special plans.
As I yet again combed my hair to hide it, I recalled my mother's words:
"Child, don't, that doesn't suit you."
"You have such a lovely high forehead, don't hide it."

He asked me to the school ball, and I was looking forward to getting to know him better, but it was too soon.
We rented a boat on Baldeney lake,
and everything was going well until I lost one of the oars.
When I tried to retrieve it, I fell out of the boat and into the water.
I couldn't swim, and by the time he realized it,
I had almost drowned. Luckily, he was a lifeguard.
In a flash, he jumped in after me and rescued me.

I had met a terrific woman.
We went out, and I was full of illusions.
We got closer, and when she undressed, I was thunderstruck:
There were tattoos of men's heads on her entire body.
There was just one spot left. Need I say more?

...this huge old building when we came home at night.
It was a post office with a big staircase.
The stories were very high, and the stairwell light had a timer.
The post always was frugal, so the timer interval was very short.
So you made it up half a stairway
before the light went out. It was wonderful!

She came down the stairs, and I stepped aside to let her by.
She did the same, and we bumped into each other.
For a short moment I felt her breasts against my body.
I was thirteen years old at the time. It was my first erotic experience.

16

It was supposed to remain secret forever. But it only lasted two weeks.
Then a boy offered me a chocolate bar, and I couldn't resist.

I thought, 'Oh, I hope he comes over to me.'
He looked like Jean Marais, and I adored Jean Marais.
I'd seen all of his films. Well, when the teacher gave the order, the boys came over, and Jean Marais came straight to me.
I was so happy, and from then on...

I met my dream man in dance class.
Oh, he looked so handsome, and he was a fantastic dancer.
That won me over right away, because dancing was my passion.
Everything was going well,
till we started learning new step combinations.
That's when the problems started.
And you won't believe it, one day he got so irritated that he just left me standing there on the dance floor and left.

The most beautiful nights are clear, starry summer nights.
When you walk home on a night like that with your girl, you show her the stars.
And the bright stars
are the big, great, long kisses...
And the constellations are the tender little kisses here and there.
So then of course, no matter how long the way home is, it seems short as you wander from constellation to constellation, and before you know it, you're home.

He had been studying in Germany
and when he returned home to Istanbul in Turkey,
he took me along and introduced me to his whole family.
He'd say, "This is my little *simiklibicek*."
"This is my little *karinca*."
I looked the words up in my dictionary.

And guess what they mean?
Simiklibicek means 'snail', and *karinca* means 'ant'.
Can you imagine? Me, who's 1.78 tall in high heels...
...a 'little ant'?

He didn't pick me up.
Furious, I really gave it to him: I put a wet sponge on his chair,
spilled cocoa on his shirt, let the air out of his tires,
faked a love letter from a fat classmate, and didn't say another
word to him.
As far as I was concerned he was dead, I was so furious.

Such bad luck: My coin fell into the drain in front of the ice-
cream parlour.
I stood there crying my eyes out,
and at that moment Helmut came out,
the tallest, best-looking boy on the whole street.
He gave me his ice-cream cone and said, "Hold it, but don't
lick it."
He tried to lift the lid of the drain, but of course he couldn't.
Then he said, "We can share my cone. You take a lick, I take
a lick."
And that was our first kiss, via a small detour.

Time was running out and we had to work through the night
to finish our paper for the seminar on fairy tales.
When she took the last page out of the typewriter,
she came over to me and gave me a kiss.
A French kiss. I was horrified.
Snow White, a French kiss? To me she was Snow White.
Nothing ever came of our relationship.
The next semester, I signed up for a different course:
The Three Penny Opera.

It was Saturday night, and I was in a terrible state.
My boyfriend and I had just split up, and you know how that is.

18

So I persuaded my sister to go to the *Turmhof* with me.
It was a fancy place, and guests had to order wine.
So we sit down at a small table and order our wine.
Then my sister says she has to go to the ladies' room.
As we walk back past the front desk,
two men approach us young things in the hotel lobby and say,
"Would you like to come upstairs with us?"
I was aghast. We were so shy about these things.
I said, "How dare you ask that?"
Then we grabbed our coats and left.
We'd gotten there at 7:30 and were gone by 8:00.

We were at a big party and danced all night till our feet were
smoking.
Around midnight we took off our shoes and threw them in
a corner.
On and on. We danced to whatever they played.
When we were ready to leave, our shoes had vanished.
They were nowhere to be found.
My girlfriend had to walk home in silk stockings.
That killed the mood, and our love, too. Maybe it was for
the best.

I can tell you one thing for a fact: I wasn't always this old.
Once when I was younger, I wanted to go on holiday with
two women.
And what happened? When we got to the parking lot,
we saw that our car had been stolen.
As we stood there, the first thought was, 'No car, no
holiday, no sea, no beach...'

Of the fifty or so students in the course, only seven were girls.
The prettiest of them was my friend, and one evening,
we walked home over the bridge, the river, broad and calm
below,

the moon above, clear, bright, and full.
My girlfriend began talking about the moon's spiritual and magic qualities
and its effect on the earth, plants, animals, etc.
All that came to my mind
were facts like its distance from Earth and how much it weighed.
That irritated her a bit.
Later I threw a matchbox in her face, and that,
along with the effect of my de-romanticizing the moon,
caused our friendship to cool off.
But then, we were three dogs fighting over a bone.
One of us helped her with her exams, the second wrote her lovely poems,
which found her favour,
and the third brought her nylons from West Berlin.
I was number three.
That just goes to show you what a woman's charms can do to a man.

*

Darling.
Darling.
Darling.
Darling.
Darling!
Darling!

Second Part

Turn!
Turn!
Turn!
Turn!

*

"The first to appear on the pond with their young
are a small, happy family of mallards.
Though they're barely a day old,
the ducklings can already swim and forage for themselves.
The mother duck keeps a strict watch
so they don't stray, and keeps them safe and warm.
White-eyed pochards mostly live east of the Elbe.
They're just visitors in the West.
The release of two pairs proved to be a success:
Nine ducklings were counted by mid-summer.
Perhaps it will be possible to reintroduce this species here.
In late summer, fall migration brings
other kinds of ducks to the pond, such as this drake...
...or this female of the same species.
A male widgeon.
Tufted ducks: the male, black-and-white, the female, dark
brown.
The young white-eyed pochards have grown up.
The first year on the new pond draws to a close.
Many wild creatures have settled and raised their young
here."

*

I can't believe it.
You know how many times we rehearsed this step?
And now it's all wrong. This can't be true!
And move it, will you! A bit faster!

This is rubbish! And I have to wear this dark dress,
this high-necked thing! I hate it!
I'd much rather have a neckline that's a bit lower.
Edith! Edith, where are you? I have to tell you something!
Edith! Where are you?
I have to tell you something!

Forty five...

Ladies and gentlemen on stage, please

Oh yes, *die Senioren, the seniors*. From January 2000 till December 2004 they had performed *Kontakthof* approximately 50 times to a more than enthusiastic audience of 50,000. The oldest member is Alfred. He is already 77 years of age. Many are in their seventies. The lady playing the lead role, Edith, is the only senior not wishing to continue. She danced her last performance with 65 years. Bravo! The remaining seniors decided to send Pina a letter: "we want to keep on dancing for you and to continue further guest touring performances of *Kontakthof*, all over the world". What effect would this letter have on me? Hopefully it won't mean I have to teach it once again right from the very beginning! I spoke with Pina. She wasn't going to say no, hinder these old people from dancing, by taking their pleasure in performing away. I should find a replacement for Edith. I must be mad, especially knowing from the first time round all the difficulties, the patience needed, how time consuming. My responsibility now, even greater still, then it meant my new candidate, Krista, not only had to learn and master dancing the lead role, she must be trained and taught so professionally that she would not stand out as being new. Krista had never been on stage in her life before. The rest of the seniors have been dancing it for almost 5 years and when I think back to the premiere of *Kontakthof* in 2000 or look back at old videos, I see huge progression in all of the seniors, in self assurance, precision, stage presence, less mistakes, technique and quality. Each is his or her own self on the Stage. Do I want to take on this responsibility? Working so close, private, getting so near to someone I yet hardly know, once again. Shall I? If no is my answer, it will mean the end of

Senioren – Kontakthof. I can't do that, I know them too well.
I said: Ok, let us continue.

＊

I was looking forward to my next tour with the seniors in
Weimar. Travelling with them is mostly good fun. One
week away from home, alone, could be just the thing to
cheer me up. Alone, is a luxury I have not treated myself to
very often.
My Hotel in Weimar, 'Grand Hotel Russischer Hof', was
just perfect. Awaiting me in my room, stood a beautiful
bowl of delicious, expensive, quality, chocolates to tempt,
I couldn't resist, and in no time had savoured all. But all!
I somehow needed that. The following day, I thanked the
Hotel Manager sincerely: "for a very special guest" he replied
with a quaint smile. I returned a sweet smile and went to
join the others at Breakfast. I asked, had they also received
chocolates? But no, only me! A very special guest indeed!
Life is full of surprises. At 3 p.m. on the day of the first performance, Margarita hurt herself. She had twisted her knee
and the doctor had forbidden her to dance. So who had to
jump in quickly? Me. Yes in *Kontakthof* I have a sort of
double function, not only with Beatrice Libonati as Rehearsal
Directress, but also as 'stand-by' for all the senior women.
I know all the parts. Just as well because at any time anything could happen with elderly people over the age of
65 years. They would rather swallow another pain killer
than miss out on a performance. On stage, me a professional dancer, performing with the seniors felt rather strange,
dancing beside, all those grey haired men and women. Oh,
please excuse. No, they are not all grey. Some women still
colour or dye. Bodies which are not perfect, crooked feet,
fat bellies, wrinkled, face and neck, legs with varicose veins,
hanging shoulders, small, tall, fat, thin, some still pretty,
others not, just average, normal, old, people, flabby arms,

false teeth. I remember during the general rehearsal in the pause correcting Alfred: "the next time you run to centre stage and bang yourself down to the kneeling position like you did tonight, you'll end up in hospital. Be careful! He started to laugh and answered in deep Wuppertal dialect: "you don't need to tell me that, Jo. When I felt my false teeth almost fall out of my mouth and land on stage, I realised for myself that I had almost overdone it". My goodness! His lovely wife, Ursula, wore, for a time during chemotherapy, a grey wig. All her beautiful, thick, wavy hair had fallen out. That's life! Only one of the senior men wears a hair piece, more so, because in younger days he suffered severe hair loss. Looks very natural and I assumed all seniors aware of this. However, one day during rehearsal, Inge, who has rather a lot of partner work with him particularly in one scene called: "sensitive to yourself and partner", where she has to touch him on the head, her suddenly turning bright red, completely embarrassed and coming over to me: "Jo, why didn't you tell me, it is a toupet". I thought she knew.

Inge is great in the performance, for a while we lost her, she had to undergo a rather big heart operation, six months later she had recovered and returned to us healthy and happy. *Kontakthof* without Inge, no thanks.

On tour with the seniors we have celebrated the best 'after show' parties I have ever celebrated. Really, laughing and dancing like teenagers till early morning hours, incredible how happy, joyful after each and every Performance, the Applause, the success, their faces radiant, utter bliss. Even though their feet may be killing from the high heeled shoes they wear during the piece, tiredness, or knowing that critics will be given next day at 11 a.m. they go on dancing, eating, and drinking and having fun until they almost cannot any more. But no one is ever drunk. It's so beautiful. Indeed, the seniors, treasuring just being alive, the moment and the right now, and their pleasure and freedom in dance. I will never forget Thea, our oldest senior woman, then 72, now 75 years of age, improvising a dance together with Anke. I had never seen anything so expressive, weird and interesting, a touch of Wigman. Professional dancers beside them would have no chance topping them.

On tour we mostly had reasonably good hotels, just once in Toulouse, France, not, tiny rooms, only showers and awful Bedspreads which when you touched them felt as if you were sleeping with a dead cat. Due to the Breakfast room also being small we decided to move all the tables together. The waitress brought us a simple French breakfast consisting of fresh, crispy, crunchy baguette and strong coffee. Hmmm delicious, I thought, as I began spreading my baguette thick with butter and jam. Suddenly I heard Anke complaining: "there is no way I can eat this white bread, I'm going up to my room to get my healthy brown German bread, which I have packed in my suitcase". Thea began to dip her baguette into her coffee. Like this she could at least eat it. Inge had given up, after cutting her gums on crisp and crunchy baguette. It was hilarious. We were all laughing and crying. If you broke it up in to little pieces and ate slowly, you could eat it. When I stood up to leave, I looked under the table. The whole floor was a mess of bread crumbs. I will never forget it.

Before each first night performance, the seniors receive a letter per fax from Pina:

You dear ones
From New York I send you all, all my love and warmest thoughts and best wishes. I wish you all a wonderful performance in Genua. I am with my whole heart with you. Dance beautifully. Good Luck.
I embrace you, with love
Your Pina.   18.11.2004

Here another one:

You beautiful ones
Not far away from you all and in the 'Lichtburg'
I will be with you and thinking dearly of you, when you
perform tonight and inspire again the people of
Wuppertal and the many friends who will be watching.
Enjoy it and be glad.
You are all so fantastic.
Toi, toi, toi.
I kiss and hug you all from my heart and with love
Always yours
Pina.   17.02.2006

How nice of her. To every first night performance, where ever we were, came almost the same words. I have collected 15 such letters. This letter from Pina then gets copied 26 times and is given to each of the seniors, for him to do with what she or he likes. Either save it, or stick in an album together with the other letters or to throw away. Pina also sends every one a Rose. Even I receive one. It is sweet of her. And she would love to *be loved* by everyone.

I find it somehow fantastic, almost crazy that I am now teaching German, so to say, children of war in dance and that 60 or 65 years thereafter. What an amazing opportunity. I come from a far away country. Australia. Australia has no where near as much history as Germany. Each one of the seniors is a human being and has his or her own life story, destiny, psycho, soul, mind, many have suffered serious, grave breakdowns to their health or been unluckily in their lives: breast cancer, heart attack, heart disorder, osteoporosis, knee operation, lymph gland cancer, high blood pressure, deaf on one ear, miscarriage, or given birth to a still born, or even witnessed their own child being run over, anything and everything, depression. That's life, old people. But this lot of seniors with whom I have been working so many years are not losers. They will not and do not give up. They say to me: "go, struggle with life". When they start talking about the War, I become all ear. Night for night escaping to the basement, fleeing, running for your life, twin brother shot dead, father missing, wounded, mother dead. Words like bombing, bunker, starvation, food ration cards, Hitler, persecution of Jews, evacuate or everything around us in flames, remain only words to me. Seen it in film, read about in books. But they know it for real. They were there. They remember it even though at the time they were only little children.

I have learnt so much about life from them, also about love and relationships. They understand me, I understand them. I mean, if I had to make a decision between Dance Theatre Pina Bausch, and my family, my answer would be, my family. My children should not have to suffer just because I work. I am not really a career woman. I just happened to love my two tracked life, torn between the Dance World and my down to earth family life. The more time I spend with the seniors and normal people, the further it seems to drag me away from dance and theatres. These days everyone seems to be calling themselves an 'artist'. Real artists I know, keep it quiet. It is more the person who interests me. How exciting it must be for the seniors, at this late day in life, finding their way around now in the Theatre World, away from everyday 'boring' life. They will remain grateful to Pina for the rest of their lives for making this dream *Kontakthof* come true. Indeed an exceptional present. One which has enriched their lives beyond anything one can think of.

I do however miss my dancing days and at times, also Pina. Sometimes I wonder if she is slowly losing her sense of Reality. Living under all that strain and responsibility, concentration, discipline, high level, the determination not to give up, one tends to forget, even Pina is getting older. Yes, she is now over 65 years. Choreography can be a nightmare. One could compare it almost to giving birth. And just how many pieces-children has Pina given us over a period of more than 30 years. It is no wonder she has difficulty in finding names for them, it can take months before a title is announced. Very exciting before a premiere is when the former Manager, Mr Schmiegelt, presents himself in front of the curtain on stage: "ladies and gentlemen, dearest public, may I please have your attention. Speaking in the name of Pina Bausch I would like to apologise. The piece which will be shown tonight is in working progress, this means if you have tickets to come again to the performance tomorrow or the day after, you may not be seeing the exact same piece which you will be seeing tonight at the premiere. A title will be given at later date. Thank you for you understanding". Wuppertals public laugh and whisper a little, as they have heard this speech over the years many times before. They do understand completely, because they know exactly any new piece of Pina Bausch is worth waiting for and because the people of Wuppertal see Pina, as 'their Pina', export article of their town, brand name of the country Germany, most desired choreograph of the world, prize winner from all prize winners for dance.

Jo Ann Endicott

If I tried concentrating on getting my arm right,
then my feet went wrong

We almost missed the audition for *Kontakthof*. My wife,
Ulla, and I were sitting having breakfast listening to the
radio-WDR 3 when we heard about Pina's new project
Kontakthof 'with seniors over 65 years of age'. What an
excellent opportunity of meeting Pina and the dancers
and perhaps acquiring a good look behind the scenes and
an even closer outlook altogether into the famous dance
company which we have been fans of since years.
On reflecting we decided to ring up the office in Wuppertal
and were told to turn up the next day. With great respect
and awe, our hearts pounding quickly, we entered the
studio called 'Lichtburg'. One hundred people were already
there. Dominique Mercy instructed our group. What an
honour! The fun soon decreased as I started to have trouble
learning the movements to the first diagonal in the second
half of the piece.
On Pina's entrance to the room I felt as if everyone had
stopped breathing. "Then show me what you have learnt
over the past few days", she said. By now I could hardly
swallow, throat dry. I had only been learning the steps since
50 minutes, the others two days longer. So we showed
her the diagonal. The closer I became to Pina, the more
mistakes I made. Ok, I said to myself. That's it! You got to
see the Lichtburg from inside and you managed a good
close look at Pina Bausch. Nice memories, and now you can
go home! As she then chose the group in which I was in:
"I'll take you all", I was near dumbfounded.
After this, the real work began. Slowly I became aware of
just how little I knew of my own body, let alone move and
control it. Our dance teachers, Ed, Beatrice and Jo showed

us some movements, which on them seemed very easy and elegant. Soon I realised that what I saw and what my brain was ready to assimilate were two different things. Learning it and repeating it, near to impossible. If I tried concentrating on getting my arm right, then my feet went wrong. Add a smile or a laugh while doing the step, then everything began to go wrong. My brain, proved forgetful, too slow to pick up, no connection between head and body. Slowly I began to understand how well trained, concentrated and highly specialised the dancers we have so often seen on stage must be. On this professional level at which we were being taught, I realised, we seniors, would never achieve. Pina said the premiere would take place in 3 months. In actual fact it took us 1 year and 3 months.

Secondly I learnt that life as a dancer has little to do with glamour and splendour. Rehearsals in the ballet studio at the opera house sounds very posh, impressing, however is not. The room was small, outdated, run down. Difficult to imagine such master works, like *Sacre* being created here. Even the 'Lichtburg' is no way, a luxury studio. It used to be a cinema, looks now like they just got rid of all the chairs, left all the glaring lights, the heating, and a new dance floor was put down.

Art is beautiful, but is a lot of hard work, said Karl Valentin. He sure was right. In the beginning we would rehearse twice a week, then four times and shortly before the premiere, every day. Same thing over and over again: placing, run through, transition, entering and exiting, till everyone understood how important discipline and precision were. Beatrice was very exact and did not tolerate any mistake. She insisted that only the correct movement was acceptable. A small crisis occurred within the group. Some of the seniors wanted Pina to adapt the *Kontakthof* a little to suit their age, after all they were amateurs and they were over 65 years. They would never be able to dance the piece like the dance

company, alone the thought of doing the obscene 'hip step'!
Beatrice was somewhat speechless over this petty quarrel.
I vehemently contradicted Alfred, found it narrow minded.
I wanted *Kontakthof* as it was and not a version of con-
venience for elderly.

And, was that all, insight into the working conditions of a
dancer? Where was all the fun, joy, excitement? We had
some of that as well. But only after success and the standing
ovations came.

I remember waiting at the door of the 'Lichtburg' before
rehearsal. Suddenly she appeared, Jo Ann Endicott. I had
read and heard so much about her, but regrettably never
seen her live on stage. Jo brought warmth and affection in
to the rehearsals.

Jo's spontaneous ideas were fun. Jo and Beatrice appeared
to the seniors like a married couple, who do not get on. Like
children in such marriages, we just wanted harmony, for
our sake. We needed them both, had no choice but learn to
deal with both temperaments.

How is it then, working with Pina Bausch, our friends
asked over and over again? Difficult to answer, she very
seldom came to our rehearsals. However when she attended,
she was friendly. Pina had bestowed the whole responsibility to Jo and Beatrice. Had she watched a rehearsal, we
received the following day from Beatrice a very, very long
list, pages and pages long of Corrections from Pina for the
seniors: Pina said this, Pina said that, etc, etc. What we then
concluded was that Pina nevertheless had the control over
everything. Once one of the parts had to be recast, this
decision was not made without Pina's consent. Photos were
faxed to New York and from there Pina decided.

Her absence proved less disturbing. Then thru working on
the piece I felt I was gradually getting to know her. Ulla and
I had seen *Kontakthof* with the Company already a few
times. Like this I surmised I knew the piece, somewhat.

32

Almost instantly I realised there were more scenes to it than I could remember. During actual rehearsing, watching and repeating I became aware how cleverly composed *Kontakthof* was, compact group arrangements, changing to solos or sudden entrance from the two girls in pink dresses. Cheerful scenes switching into sad and then simple quiet moments turning to chaotic. The music, slowly tuned down in volume and taken over by talk scenes. Sometimes the music underlies what we see on the stage, sometimes it gives a comment, it can also be sheer irony.

How effective, skilful the usage of the entire stage, in each corner, spot or place something happening. Compact diagonals, front line groups, counter movements in profile, circles, lone calm figures added to hectic, frantic. Rows of chairs being moved backwards forwards, in ever new function position. The chair in general! From back stage we hear laughing and from the ramps edge downstage one of the pink girls goes balancing. The more I understood of the piece the better I felt. And because I understood and wanted to do it exactly right I was willing to accept the sometime tiresome, repetitive rehearsals.

It shocked me when I read that the professional dancers were also performing *Kontakthof* one week before our premiere. They will steal the show from us and make us look like fools, I thought. With their young, trained, elegant and beautiful bodies what chance will we oldies, marked from our lives have? Professionals up against the non-professionals. In actual fact it turned out quite differently. Beatrice and Jo had done all they possibly could, Beatrice through her strict coaching and Jo in her faith in us. Even the Dance Company members wished us good luck. It was beautiful after the premiere when the company professionals, congratulated us on having danced their piece or that particular role which was theirs, so marvellously. Lutz Förster embraced me with his never ending long arms, congratulated me and said "it could not have been cast better". I felt honoured until I understood what he meant. The public were almost beside themselves, so much applause and rejoicing and not only from family and friends. Some of the professional dancers were so impressed, touched, that they said they did not want to dance *Kontakthof* anymore and that it belonged now to the seniors. Even on tour we have experienced so many inspired spectators and now returning to Wuppertal for performance, the amazing success remains for *Kontakthof* with seniors. Later, due to illness, I was forced to take a break. Like this I was able to see it with Ulla from the audience. We were totally impressed.

As time passed on I wished to take part again. We enquired. Soon after we were back in, the seniors greeted us with open arms. Our contact to Jo and Beatrice remained and it somehow felt like coming home.

It was nice to see that a great friendliness between Beatrice and the seniors had developed. There were private phone calls. Some attended her solo evenings. Working together and success had brought up a feeling of togetherness.

I enjoyed touring with *Kontakthof*, not because it meant getting away from home and no, I am not a great fan of group journeys at all, but because it was terribly interesting, witnessing the diverse reactions of the public in the other countries. Seeing and hearing the differences in humour, in what the French, Dutch, Italian and English laughed over, or which particular scene they were most touched by, how they expressed their feelings towards us. Surprisingly the piece was understood and appreciated everywhere. After the performance or next day in the town, we often met enthusiastic inspired people who thanked and congratulated us, especially in Italy. In Udine in front of the theatre, once again acclaim, hugs and kisses, photos and best wishes, amazing. And now, it seems all good things must come to an end.

I admire the seniors who stood it out the whole 7 years. They were the ones whom we have to thank most, and of course Beatrice and Jo. I know how much work it has taken to accomplish the end result. Being a former teacher myself, I am completely aware of what it is like having to correct the same mistakes over and over again, up against convenience, indifference, carelessness. Jo had to work so many years teaching patiently, lovingly her part to Edith, and then once again all over to Krista, after Ediths' departure. Otherwise *Kontakthof* would have come to an end.

Beatrice kept on working against the opinion of many of the seniors: we know it all now and we can do it, why still all the criticism. This is how we managed to keep *Kontakthof* alive.

To summarise, it proved an extremely, interesting, lovely, rewarding adventure for Ulla and myself. Not the fulfilment of a life time dream, and definitely not the long awaited rescue from the black hole in which many old people fall into on retirement. But we did achieve what we set out for, which was insight into the professional world of Theatre and the chance of working personally and intensely on one of the great Pina Bausch pieces called *Kontakthof*, and the great luck to have met so many dear people on our way. I must make one point clear, once a teacher always a teacher: without my wife, Ulla, I never would have done it.

*Karlheinz Buchwald**

English translation by Jo Ann Endicott.

Kontakthof

mit Damen und Herren ab „65“

Ein Stück von PINA BAUSCH

Kontakthof ist ein Ort, an dem man sich trifft,
um Kontakt zu suchen.
Sich zeigen, sich verwehren.
Mit Ängsten. Mit Sehnsüchten
Enttäuschungen. Verzweiflung.
Erste Erfahrungen. Erste Versuche.
Zärtlichkeit und was daraus entstehen kann,
war ein wichtiges Arbeitsthema.
Ein anderes, zum Beispiel, war Zirkus.
Etwas von sich selber zeigen, sich überwinden.

Kontakthof wurde zum ersten Mal 1978 in Wuppertal aufgeführt.
Danach in vielen Ländern.
Mein Wunsch, dieses Stück, dieses Thema,
auch mit Damen und Herren mit viel Lebenserfahrung zu sehen,
wurde mit der Zeit immer stärker.
So fand ich den Mut, *Kontakthof* Älteren, über ‚65', anzuvertrauen.
Wuppertalern.
Weder Schauspielern. Noch Tänzern.
Einfach Wuppertalern.

Im Februar 2000 war es dann soweit.

Zunächst sollte das Ganze einmalig sein.
Deshalb wurde dann auch eilig dieser Film gedreht.
Niemand ahnte, dass *Kontakthof mit Damen und Herren ab „65"*
in den folgenden Jahren durch viele Länder Europas reisen sollte.

Pina Bausch

38

Dialoge

Erster Teil

Guten Abend, ich komme aus Paris!
Ich komme aus Hamburg, bin verheiratet.

*

Du bist sehr schön!
Du bist sehr stark!
Du bist Spitze!

*

Er sieht aus wie ein Frosch. – Ja, und die...
Glubschaugen. – Ja, Sauerkrauthaare.
Wahrscheinlich hat sie Haarausfall.
Und ich finde, auch der Rock könnte... – Wie 'ne Kaulquappe,
wie ein Frosch.
Ja, und diese Nase. Eine Blumenkohlnase.
Ist wie zwei in einem. – Ja, genau, und diese Ohren.
Und guck mal. Nun berührt er sie auch.

Eins, zwei, drei...

Die kleinen Beine und der dicke Körper.
Und ihre aggressive Weiblichkeit.
Ob die als Kind auch schon so hässlich war?
Bestimmt. Und Sauerkrauthaare hat sie auch.

*

Ich stehe am Ende vom Klavier und drohe zu fallen.
Aber bevor ich das mache, schreie ich.
Ganz laut, damit niemand es verpasst.
Dann krieche ich unter das Klavier.

Gucke raus.
Vorwurfsvoll.
Und ich tue so, als ob ich ganz allein sein will.
Aber eigentlich möchte ich, dass jemand herkommt.
Dann nehme ich meinen Schal
und versuche, mich zu erwürgen,
in der Hoffnung, dass jemand kommt,
bevor ich tot bin.

*

Du, ich möchte gern essen gehen.
Au ja, da hätte ich auch Lust zu.
Ich lade dich ein.
Das ist nett von dir. Wo wollen wir hingehen?
Ich weiß da ein schönes Lokal. – Was ist das denn für ein Lokal?
Hier in Wuppertal? – Es ist außerhalb der Stadt.
Italienisch.
Ach nee, italienisch hab ich überhaupt keine Lust zu.
Doch. – Wollen wir nicht was Schönes, Deftiges?
Eisbein mit Sauerkraut und Kartoffelpüree.
Wir können auch was Anderes bekommen.
Gibt's da auch Pillekuchen mit Speck und Zwiebeln?
Ja, dafür müssen wir aber in die Stadt.
Oh ja, das ist vielleicht besser.
Mit Reibekuchen könnte ich was anfangen. – Reibeplätzchen mit Zucker und Zimt!
Kotelett, auch lecker, mit gekochtem Schinken.
Grünkohl, mit Kartoffeln und Speck.
Und was wollen wir als Nachtisch essen?
Milchreis mit sauren Kirschen.
Vanilleeis mit heißen Kirschen.
Ja, oder Bergische Waffeln! Wäre auch lecker.
Ja, da fällt mir aber auch Kaffee ein. Eine schöne Tasse Kaffee.

*

Aua!

*

Wo bist du?
Im Theater?
Da bin ich auch.
In der Pause werden wir uns sehen, im Foyer.
Du kommst herunter?
Wegen deines Anzugs?
Das ist doch Blödsinn.
Ich werde jeden genau ansehen. Ich werde dich erkennen.
Es sind Tänzerinnen auf der Bühne. Siehst du sie?
Was sagst du? Ich soll nicht weinen?
Wo bist du jetzt?

*

Hallo, Peter!
Hallo, Peter!
Zeig mir mal, was du gelernt hast.
Zeig mir mal den Hüftschritt, den du gelernt hast.
Nimm mal die Jacke, ich kann überhaupt nichts erkennen.
Das kann doch wohl nicht der Hüftschritt sein,
den wir so lange geprobt haben. Schau mich an.
Und rechts, und Mitte, und links, und Mitte und rechts.
Dreh dich mal zur Rückseite. Ich möchte das von hinten sehen.
Jacke hoch.
Das kann doch nicht dein Ernst sein.
Dreh dich noch mal nach vorne.
Schau mich an. Große, saftige Kreise.
Links, Mitte und rechts.
Och, Peter, das ist doch nicht so was!
Mach das mal mit Schritten nach vorne.
Och, Peter, es ist überhaupt nicht das. Wie lange hast du...?
Was hast du gemacht während der Zeit, wo wir geprobt
haben?

Du wirst es nie lernen. Du wirst noch ein Jahr brauchen.
Andreas, Musik!

*

Eins, zwei, drei...

*

Ach, war das schön.
Du, Inge, wollen wir das nicht mal in Schwarz probieren?
Oh ja, in Schwarz.
Fertig?
Andreas, Musik!
Genug. Es reicht, es ist doch nicht so schön.

*

Head.
Cheek.
Chest.
Stomach.
Knee.

*

Ich bin nicht böse, ich möchte nur alleine sein.

Na, Werner, was ist los?
Bist du mal wieder krank?

Ich bin nicht böse, ich möchte nur alleine sein.

Das wäre ja mal was ganz Neues.
Du bist nichts, hast nichts und kannst nichts.

Ursula!
Ursula!

Mein Gott, bist du jetzt etwa tot?
Wahrscheinlich noch nicht mal das. Alter Pickelheini.
Typisch. Alles steht, und du liegst.
Kein Pep, kein Temperament. Ein schlaffer Mensch.

Was macht er jetzt? Er will uns jetzt die Nase voll stinken.
Oh, der raucht.

Du bist eine Null, eine einzige Null.
Pupsig und pingelig.

Er hat schon so kleine Augen.
Er braucht ja außer seinen Zigaretten auch nix zu sehen.

Ein Leben an deiner Seite…
Aber du hast ja gar keine Seite.
Du zerquetschtes Ei. Du langweilst mich.

Er sieht aus wie ein großes Baby, findest du nicht?
Ja, die Bäckchen, die Hängebäckchen. – Und guck mal,
seine Wurstfinger…

Du bist doch nur noch ein schlechter Witz, ohne Rückgrat!

…Brötchen zu kaufen, dann hat er gleich die Würstchen.

Wie hippelig der ist. Wie so 'n Wippelsterz wippelt der da
auf seinem Stuhl rum.
Guck mal, wenn der eine Zigarette nach der anderen raucht,
dann muss ja alles im Eimer sein.

Ah, unser Mauerblümchen schleicht sich wieder an.

Guck mal, die hat die Petersilie noch in den Zähnen.
Wahrscheinlich kennt er keine…

Du bist der geborene Irrtum.

Seife auch nicht, ne?
Wenn er Seife hätte, würde er wahrscheinlich die Zähne damit...

Mein Gott, wie konnte mir das nur mit dir passieren.
Ich muss ja blind gewesen sein.

...und Unkraut auf Petersilie, und dann wäscht er sich
nicht.
So riecht es jedenfalls, ne?
Wahrscheinlich hat er eine ganze Knolle Knoblauch gegessen.
Und er hat bestimmt nie Freunde, wenn er so stinkt, ne?
Und Frühlingszwiebel. Ich glaube, das nennt man *nouvelle
cuisine*
Und Stinken macht einsam, ich sag's dir.
Ich glaube auch, so steht er auch da. Guck mal, die Strümpfe.
Wochenlang nicht gewaschen.
Ich glaube, es sind Seidenstrümpfe.
Obwohl die so schön riechen.
Wahrscheinlich ist er auch noch stolz drauf, ich sag's dir.

Werner!

Ich kann's nicht mehr aushalten. Ich muss jetzt gehen, Jutta.
Es ist so schrecklich.

Werner?
Werner?

*

*Ich lasse meinen Körper schwarz bepinseln, schwarz bepinseln
Und fahre zu den Fidschi-Inseln, zu den Fidschi-Inseln
Dort ist noch alles paradiesisch neu
Ach, wie ich mich freu, ach, wie ich mich freu*

Ich trage nur ein Feigenblatt
Mit Muscheln, Muscheln, Muscheln
Und geh mit einer Fidschi-Puppe
Kuscheln, kuscheln, kuscheln
Aus Bambus richt ich mir 'ne Klitsche ein
Ich bin ein Fidschi, will ein Fidschi sein.

*

...zwölf, dreizehn Jahre gewesen sein, und wir haben ja
immer versucht,
wir Jungens, mit den Mädchen zusammenzukommen.
Das war so schwer, links die Mädchen und rechts die Jungs
in der Schule.
Aber an einem Tag, da hieß es, wir gehen mal raus,
wir wollen mal zum Bauern aufs Land gehen, aus der Stadt raus.
Und wir hatten auch eine Aufgabe. Die Aufgabe war,
Kartoffelkäfer suchen.
Zu der Zeit damals waren die Mädchen...
Da trugen die noch schöne Kleider, schöne Blusen, schöne
Röcke.
Und als wir ausschwärmten in das Kartoffelfeld...
Die Mädchen waren vor uns, wir waren mal unbeobachtet...
Da sagten wir uns: „Jetzt aber nix wie dran vorbei."
Und dann sind wir losgerannt, da passierte es dann:
Ein Mädchen fiel nun in diesen Acker, in die Furche,
und lag da mit...

Plötzlich zog er sein Hemd aus. Der Rücken war voller
Tätowierungen.
So was hatte ich noch nicht gesehen. Da drehte ich mich um
und rannte weg.

Ich war ungefähr 18 Jahre
und hatte einen ungefähr 20 Jahre älteren Mann kennen
gelernt.

Er war mein Traummann: dunkle Augen, dunkles Haar.
Aber ich war leider nicht seine Traumfrau.
Er sagte immer zu mir: „Kind, du bist einfach zu jung für mich."

Ehe ich zum Döppersberg kam, konnte ich mich nicht entscheiden:
Soll ich zu der Dunkelhaarigen
mit den braunen Augen und der tollen Figur nach Barmen fahren
oder zu der Blonden mit den blauen Augen
und dem Lächeln im Gesicht nach Vohwinkel.
Da hab ich mir gesagt:
„Lass doch einfach die Schwebebahn entscheiden."
Die nächste Schwebebahn, die kommt, da steigst du ein, und ab!
Da hab ich schnell einen Blumenstrauß besorgt,
und dann ab in die nächste Schwebebahn.

...sollte ich dieses tief ausgeschnittene bunte
oder vielleicht doch dieses durchsichtige schwarze anziehen?
Als ich noch so überlegte, guck ich in den Spiegel und dachte:
„Das kann nicht wahr sein." Da war er wieder,
dieser Pickel, der immer dann kam, mitten auf meiner Stirn,
wenn ich was Besonderes vorhatte.
Schon wieder musste ich meine Haare in die Stirn kämmen,
damit man den nicht sah, wo meine Mutter immer sagte:
„Kind, tu das nicht, das kannst du nicht tragen.
Du hast so eine schöne hohe Stirn, du musst die Haare aus dem Gesicht..."

Und dann hat er mich zum Abschlussball eingeladen und ich freute mich schon,
dass wir uns ein bisschen näher kamen, aber es war ja noch zu früh.

Da haben wir uns dann einen Kahn gemietet auf dem Baldeneysee,
und das ging auch erst ganz gut, aber ich verlor das Ruder.
Dann wollte ich das wieder schnappen, und dann flog ich da hinterher.
Und ich konnte gar nicht schwimmen, und bis er das überhaupt mal merkte,
da war ich schon in Not. Und er war ja Rettungsschwimmer.
Und er machte kurzen Prozess, und er holte mich da wieder raus.

Ich hatte eine tolle Frau kennen gelernt.
Wir trafen uns. Ich machte mir große Illusionen.
Wir kamen uns näher.
Sie zog sich aus, und ich war wie vom Donner gerührt.
Der ganze Körper mit Männerköpfen tätowiert.
Nur noch ein Platz frei, ein Schock. Soll ich noch mehr sagen?

...wenn wir abends nach Hause kamen in dieses riesengroße Altgebäude.
Es war ein Postgebäude mit einer großen Treppe.
Die alten Stockwerke waren sehr hoch. Das war ausgestattet mit Minutenlicht.
Die Post war schon immer sparsam, hatte das auf ganz niedrig gestellt.
Also schaffte man höchstens eine halbe Treppe
und dann ging das Licht aus. Wunderbar war das.

Sie kam die Treppe herunter.
Ich trat zur Seite, um sie durchzulassen.
Sie tat das Gleiche, und wir prallten aneinander.
Für einen kurzen Augenblick spürte ich ihre Brüste an meinem Körper.
Ich war damals 13 Jahre. Es war mein erstes erotisches Erlebnis.

Es sollte ewig ein Geheimnis bleiben. Aber das hielt nur vierzehn Tage.
Dann bot mir ein Junge eine Tafel Schokolade an.
Ich wurde schwach.

Ich dachte: „Hoffentlich kommt der zu dir."
Der sah aus wie Jean Marais, und ich liebte damals Jean Marais.
Ich hatte alle seine Filme gesehen, und als die Leiterin das Kommando gab,
kamen die Jungen auf uns zu, und Jean Marais kam auf mich zu.
Ich war glücklich, und fortan...

Also ich lernte meinen Traummann in der Tanzschule kennen.
Oh, er sah so super aus und konnte fantastisch tanzen.
Damit hatte er mich sofort gewonnen, denn Tanzen war meine Leidenschaft.
Na ja, es ging auch soweit gut,
bis wir neue Schrittkombinationen lernen sollten.
Da gingen die Probleme los. Und Sie werden es nicht glauben, er war eines Tages so genervt, da ließ er mich doch glatt mitten auf der Tanzfläche stehen und verschwand.

Also die schönsten Nächte, das sind die sternenklaren Sommernächte.
Und wenn man dann mit seinem Mädchen nach Hause geht, zeigt man ihm die Sterne.
Und die großen Sterne,
das sind die dicken, schönen, langen Küsse.
Und dann natürlich die Sternzeichen, das sind die kleinen Küsschen,
die man so verteilt, und dann natürlich...
...kann der Weg noch so lang sein, der wird immer kürzer dabei,
wenn man so von Sternzeichen zu Sternzeichen wandert, und schwups, ist man zu Hause.

...und er hatte hier in Deutschland studiert, und als er dann zurückfuhr
in seine Heimat in die Türkei, nach Istanbul, da nahm er mich mit
und stellte mich der gesamten Familie vor.
Und dann sagte er immer: „Das ist meine kleine *sümüklü böcek.*"
„Das ist meine kleine *karinca.*"
Ich hab im Wörterbuch nachgeschaut. „Was mag das wohl heißen, *sümüklü böcek* und *karinca*? Und was glauben Sie, was das hieß?
Sümüklü böcek heißt ‚Schnecke‘, und *karinca* heißt ‚Ameise‘.
Können Sie sich vorstellen, bei 1,78 Meter, mit Pumps natürlich..."
„Kleine Ameise..."

...und er hat mich nicht geholt. Da hab ich's ihm gegeben:
'nen nassen Schwamm auf dem Stuhl,
Kakao übers Hemd gegossen, Luft aus 'm Moped gelassen,
'nen gefälschten Liebesbrief vom Klassenpummelchen geschrieben,
und in Deutsch kriegte er auch nix mehr von mir zu hören.
Er war für mich gestorben, ich war wütend, ganz wütend.

Ja, das war ein Malheur, direkt vor dem Eisladen
rollte mir mein Groschen in den Gully.
Ich stand da und heulte Rotz und Wasser.
In dem Moment kam Helmut aus dem Eisladen,
der größte und schönste Junge von der ganzen Straße,
reichte mir sein Hörnchen und sagte: „Da, halt mal, aber geh nicht dran."
Er versuchte den Gullydeckel zu lösen, klappte natürlich nicht.
Da sagte er: „Ach, weißt du was, essen wir das Hörnchen gemeinsam."
„Mal leckst du, mal leck ich." Das war unser erster Kuss auf Umwegen.

Die Zeit war knapp, und...
Wir mussten die ganze Nacht durcharbeiten,
um die Arbeit für das Märchenseminar fertig zu kriegen.
Und als sie die letzte Seite aus der Schreibmaschine zog,
kam sie auf mich zu und gab mir einen Kuss.
Mit Zunge. Ich war entsetzt.
Schneewittchen mit Zungenkuss. Für mich war die doch
Schneewittchen.
Aus dieser Beziehung ist dann auch nichts geworden.
Im nächsten Semester habe ich ein anderes Seminar belegt.
Dreigroschenoper.

Es war mal wieder Samstagabend, und ich hatte totalen
Liebeskummer.
Mein Freund hatte mit mir Schluss gemacht,
und ich eben auch mit ihm, und Sie wissen ja, wie das ist.
Also, ich hab meine Schwester animiert: „Komm, wir gehen
in den *Turmhof.*"
Der *Turmhof*, das war damals ein ganz tolles Lokal mit Weinzwang
und kleinen runden Tischchen. Wir haben Platz genommen,
Flasche Wein bestellt, und wie das bei Frauen so ist:
Meine Schwester sagte: „Du, ich muss mal zur Toilette."
Wir sind raus, kommen zurück, am Pförtner vorbei,
da stehen da zwei Herren und sagen zu uns jungen Blagen:
„Würden Sie vielleicht mit uns nach oben gehen?"
Ich war perplex. Damals hatten wir solch eine Scheu.
Ich hab gesagt: „Wie können Sie wagen, uns so etwas zu fragen?"
Wir haben unsere Mäntel geschnappt, sind raus,
waren um halb acht im *Turmhof*, um acht Uhr waren wir
wieder draußen.

Wir waren auf einer Riesentanzfete. Wir haben getanzt, die
ganze Nacht,
dass uns die Füße brannten. Gegen Mitternacht wurde uns
das zu doll,

da haben wir die Schuhe ausgezogen und in die Ecke gefetzt.
Dann ging's weiter und alles, was gespielt wurde, wurde getanzt.
Gegen Morgen, als wir nach Hause gehen wollten, waren
die Schuhe weg.
Wir haben gesucht, gesucht, nichts war zu finden.
Meine Freundin musste auf Seidenstrümpfen nach Hause
wackeln.
Die Stimmung war weg, die Liebe auch. Vielleicht war's gut so.

Also eins steht fest, ich war nicht immer so alt wie heute,
und in jungen Jahren wollte ich sogar mit
zwei schönen Frauen in Urlaub fahren.
Und was passierte? Wir gehen zusammen zum Parkplatz,
wir kommen da an, unser Auto ist weg, ist gestohlen.
Wir stehen da. Der erste Gedanke war:
„Kein Auto, kein Urlaub, kein Wasser, kein Strand..."

Wir waren an die 50 Leute im Seminar, darunter aber nur
sieben Mädchen.
Mit der Charmantesten von ihnen war ich befreundet.
Eines Abends gingen wir nach einer Veranstaltung über die
Elbbrücke,
unter uns der breite und ruhige Fluss, über uns der Mond,
hell, klar und rund.
Und darauf begann sie, über die spirituellen und magischen
Eigenschaften des Mondes zu reden,
über seine Wirkung auf die Erde, die Pflanzen, die Tiere und
so weiter.
Mir fiel dagegen nur ein, dass er so und so viel Kilometer
von der Erde entfernt war und ein bestimmtes Gewicht hatte.
Das hat sie leicht irritiert.
Als ich ihr später noch eine Schachtel Streichhölzer ins
Gesicht warf
und außerdem die Entromantisierung des Mondes noch
wirkte,

kühlte unsere Freundschaft etwas ab.
Allerdings waren wir auch drei Hunde an einem Knochen,
sozusagen.
Einer machte ihr die Staatsübungen, der Zweite schrieb
wunderschöne Gedichte, die sie wohlwollend zur Kenntnis
nahm,
und der andere brachte ihr die Nylonstrümpfe aus West-
berlin mit.
Der Dritte war ich. Da kann man mal sehen,
was weiblicher Charme bei Männern anrichten kann.

*

Liebling.
Liebling.
Liebling.
Liebling.
Liebling!
Liebling!

Zweiter Teil

Drehen!
Drehen!
Drehen!
Drehen!

✳

„Als erster Entennachwuchs zeigt sich auf dem neuen Teich
ein munteres Häuflein junger Stockenten.
Sie sind erst 24 Stunden alt, können aber schon hervorragend
schwimmen
und allein ihre Nahrung suchen.
Die Mutterente bewacht sie, hält sie zusammen
und bietet ihnen am Ufer Schutz und Wärme.
Die Moorenten leben vorwiegend östlich der Elbe.
Sie sind im Westen nur Gäste.
Zwei Pärchen wurden ausgesetzt. Mit Erfolg.
Im Hochsommer wurden neun Junge geführt.
Vielleicht gelingt es, diese Tauchente hier heimisch zu machen.
Zum Ende des Sommers stellten sich auf dem Vogelzug
auch andere Entenarten ein, der Tafelerpel zum Beispiel.
Oder das Weibchen, die Tafelente.
Pfeifentenerpel.
Die Reiherenten.
Schwarz-weiß mit Schopf der Erpel, dunkelbraun die Ente.
Die jungen Moorenten sind herangewachsen.
Das erste Jahr des neuen Wildteiches geht zu Ende.
Viele Tiere haben sich eingefunden. Viele haben sich vermehrt."

✳

Ich kann es nicht glauben.
Wissen Sie, wie oft wir diesen Schritt geprobt haben?
Und jetzt ist alles falsch. Das kann nicht wahr sein!

ein bisschen schneller.
Es ist Müll!
Und dann stecken sie mich noch in so ein dunkles Kleid,
bis oben hin geschlossen. Ich hasse das!
Ich hätte gerne so einen kleinen Ausschnitt.
Das wäre mir lieber.
Edith, wo steckst du? Ich hab dir was Wichtiges zu sagen.
Edith! Wo bist du? Ich hab dir was Wichtiges zu sagen.

Fünfundvierzig...

Damen und Herren auf die Bühne, bitte

Ja, ja, die *Senioren*. Von Februar 2000 bis Dezember 2004 haben wir ‚es' 69 mal gespielt vor einem mehr als begeisterten Publikum von ungefähr 50.000. Der älteste Senior, Alfred, ist 75 Jahre alt. Viele sind 70 Jahre. Edith ist die Einzige, die nicht weitermachen will. Immerhin hat sie es bis zu ihrem 65. Geburtstag getanzt. Bravo. Die restlichen *Kontakthöfler* schrieben Pina einen langen Brief: „Wir wollen weiter für dich tanzen!" Sie wollten weiter mit *Kontakthof* auf Gastspielreisen gehen. Was konnte das für mich heißen? Bloß nicht noch einmal den gleichen Prozess von vorne, das Gleiche in Grün. Ich sprach mit Pina. Sie würde nicht im Wege stehen, diesen Menschen den Spaß nicht wegnehmen, sagte sie. Ich sollte mich mit dem Geschäftsführer besprechen und eine Frau finden, die eventuell für Ediths Rolle in Frage käme. I must be mad. Denn jetzt war meine Aufgabe noch viel schwieriger. Meine neue Kandidatin muss nicht nur die Hauptrolle lernen und meistern, sie muss die Rolle so professionell einüben, dass die fehlenden fünf Jahre Praxis auf der Bühne nicht zu sehen sind. Wenn ich zurückdenke an die Premiere von *Kontakthof* oder mir alte Videos anschaue und das Können der Tänzer damals mit ihrem jetzigen vergleiche, ist es ein Riesenunterschied. Selbstsicher, präzise, fehlerfrei wie sie jetzt sind. Nach fünf Jahren ist man eben kein Laie mehr. Jeder ist jetzt sein eigenes Ich auf der Bühne. Wollte ich diese Verantwortung wieder auf mich nehmen? Noch mal so nah an eine Person heran? Wollte ich das? Wenn ich nein gesagt hätte, hätten sie nicht weitermachen können. Aus. Das kann ich den Senioren nicht antun, sie sind inzwischen auch meine Freunde. Ich machte weiter. An mir sollte es nicht scheitern.

Manchmal denke ich, ohne die Alten hätte ich meinen Kontakt zu Pina ganz verloren. Denn für das Tanztheater mache ich fast nichts mehr.

*

Eine Woche von zu Hause weg zu sein – alleine. Könnte mir gut tun. Alleinsein ist ein Luxus, der mir bisher nur selten vergönnt war.

In Weimar übernachtete ich im ‚Grand Hotel Russischer Hof‘. Am ersten Tag wartete im Zimmer eine Schale voller Qualitätspralinen auf mich. Gierig wie ein Wildschwein, aß ich alle Pralinen auf ein Mal auf. Aber alle. Eine reine Symphonie in meinem Gaumen. Ich brauchte das. Am nächsten Tag bedankte ich mich an der Rezeption: „Für ganz besondere Gäste“, lächelte mich die Frau dort an. Ich strahlte. Beim Frühstück fragte ich gleich nach, und tatsächlich: niemand anderer hatte welche bekommen, nur ich. Hoppla! Ja, zum richtigen Zeitpunkt kann Schokolade bei Frauen schöne, kleine Wunder wirken.

Wie das Leben so spielt, meldete sich Margarita am Tag der Vorstellung um 15 Uhr 30 krank. Und wer musste wohl einspringen? Wer wohl? Ich natürlich. Ja, für das Stück *Senioren-Kontakthof* bin ich nicht nur, zusammen mit Beatrice, Probenleiterin, sondern auch Ersatz für alle Frauen. In Zusammenhang mit der Probenleitung sind meine Ersatztätigkeiten ganz spannend. Es gibt einfach keine, die so schnell ‚bühnenfertig‘ sein kann wie Jo. Denn bei Senioren, die schon längst den 60. Geburtstag überschritten haben, kann es schnell passieren, dass jemand krank wird. Eine Vorstellung abzusagen, wäre ziemlich das Letzte. Eher noch eine Schmerztablette schlucken und durch. Als Tänzerin unter lauter Laien auf der Bühne zu sein, zwischen all diesen grauhaarigen Frauen und Männern – eigenartig. Doch Entschuldigung, ich korrigiere: nicht alle sind grau. Manche Frauen färben oder tönen. Körper, die nicht perfekt sind, krumme Füße, dicke Bäuche, faltige Hälse, adrige Beine, Tränensäcke, klein, groß, dick, dünn, noch schöne, nicht mehr so schöne, querbeet, eben alte Menschen. Hängende Schultern, falsche Zähne. So der Alfred, bei der Generalprobe – ich sag in der Pause zu ihm: „Alfred, wenn du so zur Bühnenmitte rennst und so abrupt mit aller Kraft zum Knien kommst, kann es sein, dass du dich danach im Krankenhaus wiederfindest – übertreibe nicht". Er fing an zu lachen und antwortete im tiefsten Wuppertaler Plattdeutsch „Das brauchst du mir nicht zu sagen, Jo, das hab' ich selber gleich gemerkt, als mein Gebiss fast aus dem Mund gefallen ist".

Oh, weia. Seine Frau Ursula trug eine Zeit lang auf der Bühne eine graue Perücke. Ihre wunderschönen, dicken, welligen grauen Haare waren ihr nach der Chemotherapie ausgefallen. Ja, so ist das. Eine Zeit lang mussten wir auf unsere Inge verzichten. Sie wurde herzkrank und hatte eine Riesenoperation vor sich. *Kontakthof* ohne Inge? Nein, danke. Strahlend und gesund kam sie wieder nach sechs Monaten. Inge ist das absolute Gegenteil einer Tänzerin. Auf der Bühne, herrlich, wunderbar.

Auf Gastspielreisen haben wir die auch tollsten Feste gefeiert. Unschlagbar. So viel gelacht, getanzt, gealbert bis in die Puppen. Bei diesen Festen, die ich miterleben durfte, konnte ich kaum mithalten – sei es die Erlösungsfreude nach dem Erfolg der gerade gespielten Vorstellung, der verdiente Applaus, das Aufatmen, wieder eine Vorstellung geschafft zu haben im hohen Alter. Die reine Glückseligkeit. Und jeder darf hier so tanzen, wie er will. Ohne Korrekturen, und obwohl ihnen die Füße wehtun und womöglich am nächsten Tag gleich wieder um 11 Kritik ist oder am Nachmittag eine Matinee, es wird getanzt bis man ins Bett fällt. Mal hat Thea, die älteste von den Frauen, mit Anke einen Tanz abgegeben, so schräg, ulkig, improvisierter Ausdruckstanz. Es zieht dir die Schuhe aus. A la Wigman.

Profitänzer daneben haben keine Chance, die zu toppen. Ja, ja, die Senioren *Kontakthöfler*. Die Freude am Tanz, am Moment, am Leben.

Auf Gastspielreisen unterwegs mit den Senioren hatten wir meistens sehr schöne Hotels. Bloß in Toulouse, Frankreich, nicht. Winzige Zimmer, raue Zudecken, die sich anfühlten, als ob man mit einer toten Katze geschlafen hätte. Da der Frühstücksraum klein war, saßen wir alle eng zusammen. Da brachte die Bedienung uns das Brot. Natürlich Baguette. Frisch, knackig, knusprig. Hmmm, lecker. Ich freute mich, fing an zu essen, das Baguette dick mit Butter beschmiert und Marmelade. Anke fing an: „Das kann ich überhaupt nicht essen, ich gehe hoch ins Zimmer und hole mein mitgebrachtes deutsches Brot". Thea tunkte ihres in den Kaffee, so wurde es wenigstens weich. Inge hatte schon aufgegeben, nachdem das Baguette ihr ins Zahnfleisch geschnitten hatte. Es war so was von knusprig und knackig! Wir waren am Heulen vor Lachen. Wenn man es in kleine Stücke brach und mit Vorsicht aß, dann konnten die Senioren das französische Frühstück in diesem Hotel in Toulouse genießen. Als ich aufstand zum Gehen, guckte ich mich um. Der ganze Boden war voller Krümel. Auf Gastspielreise kommt vor jeder Vorstellung ein Brief von Pina:

Ihr Lieben,
von New York nach Genua schicke ich Euch ganz, ganz liebe herzliche Gedanken und Grüße.
Ich wünsche Euch eine wunderbare Vorstellung.
Ich bin mit meinem Herzen bei Euch.
Macht's schön. Toi, toi, toi.
Ich umarme Euch, mit Liebe
Eure Pina   18.11.2004

Und noch einer:

Ihr lieben Schönen,
nicht weit von Euch, in der ‚Lichtburg‘, werde ich
ganz fest bei Euch sein und an Euch denken,
wenn Ihr heute wieder das Wuppertaler Publikum und
Eure vielen Freunde hier inspiriert und begeistert.
Genießt es und habt ganz viel Freude.
Ihr seid ja so toll.
Toi, toi, toi.
Ich küsse und umarme Euch
von Herzen und mit Liebe.
Immer Eure Pina.   17.02.2006

Ist doch lieb von ihr. Zu jedem Gastspiel fast immer die
gleichen Worte. Sie möchte so gerne, dass sich alle von ihr
persönlich geliebt fühlen. Ich habe 15 solche Briefe auf-
gehoben. Der Brief wird 26mal kopiert, und wer will,
nimmt sich einen, bewahrt ihn auf, klebt ihn in ein Album
zu den anderen oder schmeißt ihn später weg. Rosen werden
auch verschickt. Eine für jeden. Auch ich bekomme eine.
Ja, die Pina. Sie möchte so gerne von allen *geliebt* werden.
Wer will das nicht?
Ich finde das irre, dass ich sie – sozusagen die Kriegskinder
– im Tanz unterrichten darf – und das 60 oder 65 Jahre
später. Ich komme aus einem fernen Land. Australien.
Australien hat nicht so viel Geschichte wie Deutschland.
Alle diese Senioren sind Menschen und haben ihren eigenen
Lebenslauf, ihr Schicksal, Psyche, Seele, Gesundheits-
zustand. Viele haben schwere gesundheitliche Einbrüche
und Schicksalsschläge hinter sich – Brustkrebs, Herz-
probleme, Angina pectoris, Lymphdrüsenkrebs, Osteo-
porose, Hüft-Gelenk Schmerzen, Grauer Star, Tinnitus bis
Taubheit auf einem Ohr, Fehlgeburt, Totgeburt, Kinder

gestorben, alles mögliche, klar, alte Menschen halt. Aber die Senioren mit denen ich jetzt zu tun habe, geben nicht auf. „Auf in des Lebens Kampf, Jo". Das sagen sie zu mir.

Wenn die Senioren mir vom Krieg erzählen, bin ich ganz Ohr. Nacht für Nacht im Keller, flüchten müssen, Zwillingsbruder im Krieg gefallen, Vater weg, Mutter gestorben. Worte wie Bombardierung, Bunker, Verhungern, Lebensmittelkarten, Judenverfolgungen, Hitler, Evakuierung – alles brannte um uns herum. Ich kenne es nur aus Filmen. Die kennen es aber in echt. Halt Kriegskinder.

Ich lernte ständig von ihnen. Dinge übers reale Leben. Auch über Depressionen und Beziehungen. Über die Liebe hin – die Liebe her. Ich denke, die können mein Leben besser nachvollziehen. Weil sie ganz normale Menschen sind. Ich meine, wenn ich entscheiden müsste zwischen Tanztheater oder meiner Familie, ist ganz klar, wie die Antwort lautet: meine Familie steht an erster Stelle. Meine Kinder sollen nicht leiden müssen oder zu kurz kommen, nur weil ich arbeite. Ich nehme alles auf mich, solange ich kann. Ein Leben auf zwei Spuren. Alltägliches, erdverbundenes Familienleben ist ganz normal, gar nicht glamourös! Je mehr Zeit ich mit den Senioren oder mit anderen normalen Menschen verbringe, umso mehr entfremde ich mich von meinem Tänzerleben und vom Theaterleben. Heutzutage ist sowieso jeder ein Künstler oder eine Künstlerin. Ich kann dieses Wort kaum noch hören. ,Lebenskünstler' vielleicht, oder auch nicht. An erste Stelle ist es der Mensch, der mich interessiert.

Trotzdem wie spannend für die *Kontakthöfler*, jetzt in die Theater-Welt eintauchen und reinschnuppern zu dürfen, „Auf die Bühne, bitte", und aus dem Alltagstrott raus. Dafür, dass Pina ihnen vor sechs Jahren ermöglichte, ihren Traum zu verwirklichen, sind sie ihr ewig dankbar. Letztendlich ein unvorstellbares Geschenk. Eine Bereicherung für die *Kontakthöfler* sondergleichen.

Ich vermisse den Tanz. Manchmal auch Pina. Manchmal denke ich sogar, dass Pina ‚menschenfremd' geworden ist. Wahrscheinlich liegt es an der enormen Verantwortung, die sie trägt und an dem Nicht-Aufgeben-Wollen. Hoch konzentriert schafft sie Tag für Tag weiter, Nacht für Nacht. Das, was sie will, das will sie, und sie ist nicht glücklich oder zufrieden, bis sie es hat. Jede ihrer Choreographien muss für sie ein Art Albtraum sein. Dieses Niveau zu halten. Jedes Stück wie eine Geburt. Und wie viele Stücke / Kinder hat sie uns geschenkt, in über mehr als 30 Jahren? Tanz-theater-Abende erst Monate nach der Premiere zu taufen. Ist immer spannend, wenn vor einer Premiere ein Herr zu Beginn vor den Vorhang tritt und eine kleine Rede an das Publikum hält. „Meine Damen und Herren, liebe Zuschaue-rinnen und Zuschauer, im Namen von Pina Bausch bitte ich sie um Entschuldigung. Das Stück, das sie heute Abend sehen, ist noch im Arbeitsprozess, d. h. wenn Sie morgen oder übermorgen oder überübermorgen noch einmal in die Vorstellung kommen, dann ist das Stück womöglich nicht dasselbe Stück, das sie heute Abend zur Premiere zu sehen bekommen. Ein Titel wird erst zu einem späteren Termin bekannt gegeben. Bitte haben sie Verständnis." Das Wupper-taler Publikum lacht meistens. Die kennen diese Rede vom Herrn Geschäftsführer des Tanztheaters nur zu gut, weil es oft während der letzten Jahre so war. Und die haben großes Verständnis dafür, weil es sich lohnt zu warten und eben weil sie Wuppertals Pina Bausch ist. Exportartikel der Stadt Wuppertal. Markenzeichen für Deutschland. Begehrteste Choreographin der Welt. Preisträgerin aller Preisträger für Tanz.

Jo Ann Endicott

Konzentrierte ich mich auf den Arm, stand der Fuß falsch

Beinahe hatten wir ihn verpasst, den *Kontakthof*. Ulla und ich saßen beim Frühstück, und das Radio berichtete von einem neuen Projekt von Pina Bausch: *Kontakthof* für Damen und Herren ab 65. Wir wurden blass vor Enttäuschung. Da hätten wir die Gelegenheit gehabt, Pina und ihre Tänzerinnen und Tänzer zu treffen, hinter die Kulissen zu schauen, Einblick zu gewinnen. Genau bei dem Tanztheater, das wir seit Jahren besuchten und von dem wir alle Stücke kannten. Als wir zur Besinnung kamen, riefen wir in Wuppertal an, man sagte uns, wir könnten am nächsten Tag kommen. Mit Ehrfurcht und Herzklopfen betraten wir die Lichtburg. Da waren schon über 100 Menschen. Unsere Gruppe wurde von Dominque Mercy angeleitet. Welch ein Freude und Ehre! Allerdings währte die Freude nicht lange. Ich fand die Bewegungen zur 1. Diagonalen sehr schwierig und war völlig verzweifelt, dass ich die Figuren zu Beginn des zweiten Teils nicht mal richtig erkennen konnte.

Dann betrat Pina den Raum. Alle hielten den Atem an. „Dann zeigen Sie mal, was sie in den letzten Tagen geübt haben", sagte sie. Mir stockte der Atem. Nach 50 Minuten Proben war hier jetzt Vortanzen, und die anderen hatten schon zwei Tage geübt. Ich war dann auch schlecht bei der Diagonalen, und je näher ich Pina kam, desto schwerer wurden meine Arme. Ok, sagte ich mir. Das war's. Du hast die Lichtburg von innen gesehen, du warst Pina nahe. Das gibt schöne Erinnerungen. Als sie dann die Gruppe auswählte, in der ich war („Ich nehm Sie alle"), konnte ich es nicht fassen.

Und nun begann eine Zeit, in der ich viel erlebt und gelernt habe. Zunächst etwas, was ich gar nicht wissen wollte:

wie wenig ich meinen Körper bewegen und kontrollieren konnte. Die Tänzer und Tänzerinnen, die uns trainierten, Ed, Beatrice und Jo, machten etwas vor, das leicht und elegant aussah. Ich merkte bald, dass meine Wahrnehmung und mein Gehirn nicht gelernt hatten, solche Bewegungen überhaupt genau zu erkennen. Und dann das Nachmachen. Konzentrierte ich mich auf den Arm, stand der Fuß falsch. Dachte ich ans Lächeln, machte ich falsche Bewegungen. Auch schien in meinem Gehirn die Synapsenbildung nicht so zu sein, dass ich diese Bewegungen gut behalten konnte. Mir wurde langsam klar wie gut trainiert, konzentriert und hoch spezialisiert die Tänzerinnen und Tänzer sind, die wir auf der Bühne gesehen und – wohl zu recht – bewundert hatten. Auch, dass ich und wir alle das nicht erreichen würden, was die Profis zeigten, auch das wurde mir klar. Pina hatte gesagt, in 3 Monaten solle Premiere sein. Es dauerte dann aber 1 Jahr und 3 Monate.

Das Zweite, das ich lernte, war, dass Glanz und Glamour nur ein kleiner Teil des Lebens am Tanztheater sind. Proben im Ballettsaal des Opernhauses. Das hört sich vornehm an. Der Raum war aber ziemlich klein und abgewirtschaftet. Dass dort ein Stück wie *Sacre* entstanden sein soll. Nicht zu glauben! Auch die Lichtburg ist kein Luxusort. Ein altes Kino, Stühle raus, Ballettplane rein und Lampen. Fertig. Kunst ist schön, macht aber viel Arbeit, sagte Karl Valentin. Recht hatte er. Wir probten erst zwei Mal in der Woche, dann vier Mal und vor der Premiere jeden Tag. Natürlich immer wieder dasselbe: Platzierungen, Abläufe, Übergänge, Auftritte. Bis allen klar wurde, Genauigkeit und Disziplin sind nötig, sonst geht nichts. Und da war Beatrice genau und unnachgiebig. Sie bestand darauf, dass nur das Richtige richtig war. Deshalb gab es eine große Krise, die in der Forderung der Senioren gipfelte, Pina sollte das Stück ändern. Wir seien ja schließlich Amateure und alt, da könnten wir eben nicht alles so machen wie die Kompanie, schon gar nicht diesen obszönen Hüftschritt. Beatrice sah sich aufbegehrenden Mitarbeitern gegenüber und war sprachlos. Ich fand diese Forderungen kleinkariert. Ich wollte den *Kontakthof* und nicht eine Version für Bequeme.

War das schon alles? Einsicht in die Arbeitsbedingungen professioneller Tänzer? Wo bleiben der Spaß, die Freude, die Euphorie? Die gab's auch. Die gab es auch, aber erst, als sich der Erfolg einstellte.

Einmal, ich wartete vor der Probe in der Lichtburg in der Nähe der Tür, da war sie plötzlich da, Jo Ann Endicott. Ich hatte sie noch nie gesehen, hatte aber viel über sie gelesen und schon oft bedauert, dass ich sie nicht auf der Bühne erlebt hatte.

„Jo Ann Endicott!" rief ich voller Überraschung. Sie sah mich mit ihren hellen, blauen Augen an und nahm mich in den Arm. Mein Herz hüpfte. Ich war auch stolz, dass ich sie als erster begrüßt hatte. Kurz darauf machte ich ein Foto von ihr, um den Moment nicht zu vergessen. Jo brachte Wärme und Herzlichkeit in die Proben. Ihre spontanen Einfälle machten immer Spaß. Wenn sie Edith und später Christa Korrekturen gab, ich habe es so gerne gesehen und immer für eine kleine Vorstellung innerhalb der Probe genommen. Und mir wurde auch langsam klar, dass es ihre, die von ihr entwickelte Rolle war. Jos Übermut, ihre Herzlichkeit, ihre Verletzbarkeit, ihre Kraft waren darin. Und nach und nach konnte ich mir vorstellen, wie der *Kontakthof* mit ‚der Endicott' mal ausgesehen hat.

„Wie ist es denn mit Pina Bausch zu arbeiten?" fragten unsere Freunde Ulla, meine Frau, und mich immer mal wieder. Das wussten wir natürlich nicht, denn sie kam nur wenige Male, war sehr freundlich. In der nächsten Probe dann brachte Beatrice einen Packen Korrekturen mit nach dem Motto. Pina hat gesagt... Was wir gemerkt haben, ist, dass Pina alles kontrolliert. Als einmal eine Rolle umbesetzt werden sollte, trafen nicht Beatrice und Jo die Entscheidung, die vier Mal wöchentlich mit uns arbeiteten. Es mussten Bilder nach New York gefaxt werden, und Pina entschied.

Obwohl Pina meist abwesend war, habe ich mich doch die ganze Zeit mit ihr beschäftigt, nämlich durch das Stück *Kontakthof*. Zu Beginn dachte ich, ich kenne das Stück. Ulla und ich hatten es schließlich ein paar Mal gesehen. Zuerst merkte ich, dass es viel mehr Szenen hatte, als ich erinnerte. Dann wurde mir beim Proben und beim Zusehen allmählich klar, wie klug das Stück komponiert ist. Kompakte Ensembleaufstellungen wechseln mit Solos oder Auftritten der rosa Mädchen. Heitere Szenen wechseln mit traurigen, geordnete mit chaotischen. Musik wird durch Sprechen abgelöst. Später erkannte ich, dass die Musik manchmal die Stimmung unterstreicht, manchmal die Vorgänge auf der Bühne konisch kommentiert oder auch einen Kontrapunkt setzt. Eine spannende Sache. Zuletzt verstand ich, wie geschickt Pina den gesamten Bühnenraum nutzt. Auf jeder Stelle in jeder Ecke passiert mal was. Kompakte Diagonalen, frontale Blöcke, Gegenbewegungen im Profil. Dazu die quirligen und ruhigen Einzelfiguren. Stuhlreihen aus dem Bühnengeviert wandern in immer neuen Funktionen nach vorne, nach hinten. Überhaupt der Stuhl! Noch bis hinter die Bühne führt ein Lachen, über die Rampe hinaus geht ein rosa Mädchen. Je mehr ich erkannte, desto wohler fühlte ich mich in dem Stück. Und weil ich es verstand, wollte ich auch, dass wir es genau machten, und ich akzeptierte die manchmal mühseligen Wiederholungen in den Proben.

Ich war erschreckt, als ich las, dass eine Woche vor unserer Premiere, die Kompanie auch den *Kontakthof* aufführte. Die stehlen uns die Schau, die machen uns lächerlich, waren meine Gedanken. Die trainierten, jungen, eleganten Körper mit der Bühnenerfahrung gegen uns Alte mit den Spuren des Lebens. Die Profis gegen die Non-Professionals. Es kam dann ganz anders, aber das konnten wir nicht wissen. Vor der Premiere haben uns Beatrice und Jo sehr geholfen. Beatrice durch strenge Korrekturen, Jo dadurch, dass sie zeigte, dass sie an uns glaubte. Auch die Kompanie mit ihrem toi, toi, toi und mit ihren Wünschen stärkte uns. Und es war besonders schön, dass nach der Aufführung die Profis den Senioren, die ihre Rolle gespielt hatten, gratulierten. So hatte ich die Freude, von den langen Armen Lutz Försters umschlungen zu werden. Gratulation und die beste Besetzung, die ich mir denken kann, sagte er zu mir. Ich war stolz, bis ich am nächsten Tag verstand, was er gemeint hatte. Den Jubel des Publikums bei der Premiere konnten wir alle nicht begreifen. Ich dachte, da jubeln ja nur Freunde und Verwandte. Auch dass einige Tänzer der Kompanie sagten, sie seien ganz ergriffen gewesen und sie wollten nun das Stück nicht mehr machen, glaubte ich nicht. Aber der Jubel blieb ja. Auf den Gastspielreisen und auch nach 6 Jahren 2006 in Wuppertal. Erst nachdem ich wegen Krankheit ausgeschieden war und das Stück mit Ulla anguckte, konnte ich die Wirkung verstehen.

Der Wunsch wieder mitzumachen wuchs mit der Zeit. Die Anfrage, ob wir einspringen würden, hat uns gefreut, und schließlich haben wir wieder mitgemacht. Die Senioren haben uns die Rückkehr leicht gemacht. Der Kontakt mit Jo und Beatrice war locker erhalten geblieben, und so war es eine Rückkehr ,nach Hause'.

Es war schön zu sehen, dass zwischen Beatrice und den Senioren eine große Freundlichkeit und Verbundenheit entstanden war. Man rief sich zwischendurch an. Viele besuchten Beatrices Solo-Abende. Die gemeinsame Arbeit und die Erfolge hatten zu einem Gefühl der Zusammengehörigkeit geführt.

Die Gastspiele habe ich genossen. Nicht wegen des Verreisens, ich bin überhaupt kein Freund von Gruppenreisen. Wegen der verschiedenen Reaktionen des Publikums. Es war spannend zu sehen und hören, worüber Franzosen, Niederländer oder Italiener lachen, was sie betroffen macht und wie sie ihre Freude äußern. Das hat sehr interessante Nuancen. Aber eigentlich war es sehr erstaunlich, dass das Stück überall verstanden und geschätzt wurde. Auch die Reaktionen nach der Vorstellung und am nächsten Tag in der Stadt waren sehr zu Herzen gehend. Da waren die Italiener besonders offen und herzlich. In Udine gab es nach der Vorstellung vor dem Theater noch einmal Applaus. Am nächsten Morgen in der Stadt wurden wir umarmt und geküsst, fotografiert und beglückwünscht. Jetzt geht die Zeit zu Ende. Ich bewundere die Senioren, die die ganze Zeit dabei waren. Sie haben natürlich geholfen, dass der *Kontakthof* so lange lief. Ich weiß, wie viel Arbeit Beatrice und Jo geleistet haben. Ich war ja Lehrer und kenne die Mühe, immer wieder die gleichen Fehler zu sehen und korrigieren zu müssen. Ich verstehe, wie viel Kraft es kostet, gegen Bequemlichkeit und Sorglosigkeit anzuarbeiten. Jo musste ihre Rolle lange Zeit intensiv mit Edith trainieren. Sie musste dann mit Christa noch einmal von vorne anfangen, damit der *Kontakthof* weiterlaufen konnte. Beatrice musste gegen die Einstellung der Senioren anarbeiten: „Dass kennen wir doch alles, das können wir doch alles". So blieb der *Kontakthof* lebendig.

Es war eine schöne, eine interessante Zeit für mich und Ulla. Nicht die Erfüllung eines Lebenstraums, nicht die Errettung aus dem schwarzen Loch, in das man nach der Pensionierung fällt. Aber ein großes Glück, Einblick in professionelle Theaterarbeit zu bekommen und sich intensiv mit dem Werk von Pina Bausch zu beschäftigen. Dass wir dabei liebe Menschen kennen gelernt haben, ist ein Glück. Und es war ein Geschenk, dass ich das alles mit Ulla zusammen erfahren konnte.

Karlheinz Buchwald

Kontakthof

avec des dames et messieurs au-dessus de «65» ans

Une pièce de PINA BAUSCH

Texte français de Bénédicte Billiet

Kontakthof est un lieu où l'on se rencontre,
pour chercher contact.
Se montrer, se défendre.
Avec angoisses. Avec désirs.
Déceptions. Désespoir.
Premières expériences. Premiers essais.
La tendresse, et ce qui peut de là surgir,
était un thème de travail important.
Le cirque, par exemple, en était un autre.
Montrer quelque chose de soi, se surmonter.

Kontakthof fut représenté pour la première fois en 1978 à Wuppertal.
Après, dans de nombreux pays.
Mon souhait de voir cette pièce, ce thème,
avec des dames et des messieurs ayant beaucoup vécu
se renforça avec le temps.
J'ai donc trouvé le courage de confier *Kontakthof* à des per-
sonnes de plus de ‹ 65 ›.
Des gens de Wuppertal.
Pas des acteurs. Ni des danseurs.
Simplement des gens de Wuppertal.

Le souhait devint réalité en février 2000.

Initialement il s'agissait d'un événement unique.
C'est pourquoi ce film a été tourné rapidement.
Personne ne se doutait que *Kontakthof avec des dames et des
messieurs au-dessus de «65» ans* allait voyager à travers de
nombreux pays d'Europe au cours des années qui suivirent.

Pina Bausch

Dialogues

Première Partie

Bonsoir, je viens de Paris !
Je viens de Hambourg, je suis mariée.

*

Tu es très beau !
Tu es très fort !
Quelle classe !

*

Il a l'air d'une grenouille. – Oui, et ces...
...yeux globuleux. – Oui, des cheveux filasse.
Elle perd ses cheveux probablement.
Et je trouve que la robe pourrait... – Comme un têtard, une grenouille.
Oui, et ce nez. Comme un chou-fleur.
Il y en a deux en un. – Oui, certes, et ces oreilles.
Et regarde. Maintenant il la touche.

Un, deux, trois...

Les petites jambes et le gros corps.
Et sa féminité agressive.
Tu crois qu'enfant elle était déjà si laide ?
Sûrement. Et elle a aussi les cheveux filasse.

*

Je me tiens au bord du piano et menace de tomber.
Mais avant de le faire, je crie.
Très fort, pour que tous l'entendent.
Puis je me glisse sous le piano.

Je regarde.
Avec reproche.
Et je fais comme si je voulais être toute seule.
Mais en fait j'aimerais que quelqu'un vienne.
Puis je prends mon écharpe,
et j'essaie de m'étrangler,
dans l'espoir que quelqu'un vienne,
avant que je ne sois morte.

*

Je voudrais bien aller dîner.
Oh oui, moi aussi.
Je t'invite.
C'est gentil. Où allons-nous ?
Je connais un bon endroit. – Lequel ?
Ici à Wuppertal ? – C'est en dehors de la ville.
Un italien.
Ah non, je n'ai pas envie de cuisine italienne.
Mais si. – Non, plutôt des plats bien de chez nous ?
Du jarret, avec de la choucroute et de la purée.
On peut aussi prendre autre chose.
Est-ce qu'il y a aussi des Pillekuchen avec du lard et des
oignons ?
Alors il faut qu'on aille en ville.
Oh oui, c'est peut-être mieux.
Pourquoi pas des Reibekuchen. – Oui, avec du sucre et de
la cannelle !
Une côtelette, c'est bon aussi, avec du jambon cuit.
Du chou, des pommes de terre et du lard.
Et qu'est-ce qu'on prend pour le dessert ?
Du riz au lait avec des griottes.
De la glace vanille aux cerises chaudes.
Oui, ou bien des gaufres ! C'est bon aussi.
Oui, et je pense aussi au café. Une bonne tasse de café.

*

Aïe!

*

Où es-tu?
Au théâtre?
Moi aussi.
Nous nous verrons à l'entracte, au foyer.
Tu vas descendre?
À cause de ton costume?
Mais c'est ridicule.
Je vais te chercher. Je vais te reconnaître.
Il y a des danseuses sur scène. Tu les vois?
Que dis-tu? Je ne dois pas pleurer?
Où es-tu maintenant?

*

Peter!
Peter!
Montre-moi ce que tu as appris.
Le pas avec les hanches, que tu as appris.
Soulève ta veste, sinon je ne vois absolument rien.
Et ça, ça serait le pas avec les hanches,
celui qu'on a répété si longtemps. Regarde-moi.
Et à droite, au milieu, et à gauche, au milieu, et à droite.
Tourne-toi. Je voudrais voir ça de dos.
Lève ta veste.
Tu n'es pas sérieux, non?
Tourne-toi vers l'avant.
Regarde-moi. Des cercles, grands, amples.
À gauche, au milieu, à droite.
Oh, Peter, mais ce n'est pas comme ça!
Fais-le avec des pas en avant.
Peter, ce n'est pas du tout ça. Ça fait combien de temps que tu...?
Qu'as-tu fait tout le temps où nous avons répété?
Tu n'y arriveras jamais. Tu vas encore mettre un an.

Andreas, musique !

*

Un, deux, trois...

*

Ah, c'était bien.
Inge, si on essayait en noir ?
Oh oui, en noir.
Prêts ?
Andreas, musique !
Ça suffit. Non, ce n'est pas aussi bien.

*

Head.
Cheek.
Chest.
Stomach.
Knee.

*

Je ne suis pas fâchée, je veux seulement être seule.

Eh bien, Werner ? Encore malade ?

Je ne suis pas fâchée, je veux seulement être seule.

Ça serait nouveau, ça.
Tu n'es rien, tu n'as rien, tu ne sais rien.

Ursula !
Ursula !

Mon dieu, tu es mort, à présent ?
Peut-être même pas ça. Vieux boutonneux.

Typique. Tous debout et toi, par terre.
Pas de peps, pas de tempérament. Un vrai mollasson.

Qu'est-ce qu'il fait ? Il veut nous empester.
Oh, il fume.

Tu es nul, rien que nul.
Péteux et vétilleux.
Ses yeux sont si petits.
Il n'a pas besoin de voir autre chose que ses cigarettes.
Les gens avec de petits yeux sont méchants.

Une vie à ton côté... Mais tu n'as même pas de côté.
Œuf écrasé. Tu m'ennuies.

Il a l'air d'un gros bébé, tu ne trouves pas ?
Oui, les joues, les bajoues. – Et regarde, ses doigts en saucisses...

Tu n'es qu'une mauvaise blague sans échine !

...achète des petits pains, alors il a aussi les saucisses.
Il est si nerveux. Il se trémousse comme une bergeronnette
sur sa chaise.
Regarde, s'il fume une cigarette après l'autre,
c'est que rien ne va plus.

Ah, notre fleur bleue s'en mêle.

Regarde, elle a encore du persil entre les dents.
Probablement qu'il ne sait pas...

Tu es l'erreur née.

Le savon non plus, non ?
S'il avait du savon il se brosserait les dents avec...

Mon dieu, comment est-ce que ça a pu m'arriver.
J'ai dû être aveuglée...

...et des herbes et du persil, et en plus il ne se lave pas.
On le sent, en tout cas ?
Il a probablement mangé toute une tête d'ail,
Il n'a sûrement pas d'amis s'il pue autant, non ?
Et des petits oignons. Je crois qu'on appelle ça *nouvelle cuisine*.
Puer rend solitaire, crois-moi.
Oui, ça en a l'air. Regarde, les chaussettes.
Pas lavées depuis des semaines.
Je crois que ce sont des bas de soie.
Normalement ils sentent bon.
Probablement qu'il en est fier, c'est moi qui te le dis.

Werner !

Je n'en peux plus. Il faut que je sorte, Jutta.
C'est terrible.

Werner ?
Werner ?

*

Ich lasse meinen Körper schwarz bepinseln, schwarz bepinseln
Und fahre zu den Fidschi-Inseln, zu den Fidschi-Inseln
Dort ist noch alles paradiesisch neu
Ach, wie ich mich freu, ach, wie ich mich freu
Ich trage nur ein Feigenblatt
Mit Muscheln, Muscheln, Muscheln
Und geh mit einer Fidschi-Puppe
Kuscheln, kuscheln, kuscheln
Aus Bambus richt ich mir 'ne Klitsche ein
Ich bin ein Fidschi, will ein Fidschi sein.

*

...devais avoir douze ou treize ans, et on essayait toujours, nous les garçons, de rencontrer les filles.
Mais à l'école, c'était les filles à gauche et les gars, à droite.
Mais un jour, on nous dit qu'on va sortir,
qu'on va aller à la ferme à la campagne, sortir de la ville.
Et on avait aussi une tâche. C'était de chercher les doryphores.
En ce temps-là, les filles étaient...
Elles portaient de beaux vêtements, de belles blouses, de belles jupes.
Et quand nous nous sommes égayés dans le champ de pommes de terre...
Les filles étaient devant nous, nous n'étions pas observés...
Alors nous nous sommes dit: «C'est le moment où jamais.»
Et alors nous avons couru, et là c'est arrivé:
Une fille est tombée dans ce champ, dans le sillon,
elle était allongée là...

Tout à coup, il a enlevé sa chemise. Le dos était plein de tatouages.
Je n'avais jamais vu ça. Je me suis retournée et j'ai couru.

J'avais environ dix-huit ans
et j'avais rencontré un homme de vingt ans mon aîné.
C'était l'homme de mes rêves: des yeux sombres, des cheveux foncés.
Malheureusement je n'étais pas la femme de ses rêves.
Il disait toujours: «Mon enfant, tu es trop jeune pour moi.»

J'étais presque arrivé à Döppersberg, et je ne m'étais toujours pas décidé:
dois-je rendre visite à la brunette
aux yeux marron et à la belle silhouette, à Barmen,
ou à la blonde aux yeux bleus
et au franc sourire, à Vohwinkel.
Alors je me suis dit:

« Laisse le train décider. »
Tu montes dans le premier train qui arrive, et hop!
J'ai vite acheté un bouquet de fleurs
et hop! dans le train.

...dois-je porter la robe colorée au décolleté plongeant
ou bien plutôt la noire transparente?
Alors que je réfléchissais, je regarde dans le miroir:
« Ah non, ce n'est pas vrai. » Il était là de nouveau,
ce bouton qui apparaissait toujours au milieu du front,
quand j'avais des projets particuliers.
Je devais de nouveau coiffer mes cheveux sur le front,
pour le cacher, alors que ma mère disait toujours:
« Non, mon enfant, ça ne te va pas.
Ton grand front est si beau, tu dois dégager ton visage...»

Et alors il m'a invitée au bal et je me réjouissais déjà,
car nous nous rapprochions un peu, mais c'était encore trop tôt.
Alors nous avons loué un canot au lac de Baldeney,
et d'abord ça allait très bien, mais j'ai perdu la rame.
Alors j'ai voulu la rattraper, et je me suis retrouvée dans l'eau.
Et je ne savais pas nager, et le temps qu'il le réalise,
j'étais déjà en péril. Et il était sauveteur.
Et il n'a fait ni une ni deux, et m'a sortie de là.

J'avais fait la connaissance d'une très belle femme.
Nous nous sommes rencontrés. Je me faisais de grandes
illusions.
Nous nous sommes approchés.
Elle s'est déshabillée, et j'ai été comme frappé par la foudre.
Tout le corps tatoué de têtes d'hommes.
Plus qu'une place libre, un choc. Dois-je en dire plus?

...quand on rentrait le soir dans cet immense édifice ancien.
C'était un bâtiment de la poste avec un grand escalier.

Les étages étaient très hauts. C'était équipé d'une minuterie.
La poste, qui était déjà économe, l'avait réglée très courte.
Alors on montait au maximum un demi-étage
et la lumière s'éteignait. C'était merveilleux.

Elle descendait les escaliers.
Je me suis effacé, pour la laisser passer.
Elle a fait de même, nous avons buté l'un contre l'autre.
Pendant un instant, j'ai senti ses seins contre mon corps.
J'avais alors treize ans. C'était ma première expérience érotique.
Ça devait rester secret pour toujours. Mais ça n'a tenu que
quatorze jours.
Un garçon m'a proposé une tablette de chocolat.
J'ai faibli.

Je pensais : « Pourvu qu'il vienne vers toi. »
Il ressemblait à Jean Marais, et j'adorais Jean Marais.
J'avais vu tous ses films, et quand la directrice a donné le signal,
les garçons sont venus vers nous, et Jean Marais est venu
vers moi.
J'étais heureuse, et dès lors...

J'ai rencontré l'homme de mes rêves à l'école de danse.
Oh, il avait fière allure et dansait superbement.
J'ai été tout de suite séduite, car danser, c'était ma passion.
Bon, ça a bien été,
jusqu'à ce que nous apprenions de nouveaux pas.
Alors les problèmes ont commencé. Et vous n'allez pas le croire,
un jour, il était si énervé, qu'il m'a abandonnée
au milieu de la piste de danse et a disparu.

Les plus belles nuits, ce sont les nuits d'été étoilées.
Et alors quand on rentre avec son amie,
on lui montre les étoiles.
Et les grandes étoiles,

ce sont les gros, beaux, et longs baisers.
Et bien sûr les constellations, ce sont les petits baisers
que l'on donne, et alors bien sûr...
...le chemin peut bien être long, il semble toujours plus court,
quand on va de constellations en constellations,
et hop ! on est à la maison.

...il avait étudié en Allemagne lorsqu'il est retourné
chez lui en Turquie, à Istanbul, il m'a emmenée
et m'a présentée toute sa famille.
Et il disait toujours : « C'est mon petit *sümüklü böcek*. »
« C'est ma petite *karinca*. »
J'ai ouvert le dictionnaire. Qu'est-ce que ça signifie,
sümüklü böcek et *karinca* ? Et qu'est-ce que vous croyez ?
sümüklü böcek signifie ‹ escargot ›, et *karinca* signifie ‹ fourmi ›.
Vous vous imaginez, moi, un mètre soixante-dix-huit, avec
talons bien sûr...
« Une petite fourmi... »

...et il n'est pas venu me chercher. Alors je lui en ai fait voir :
une éponge mouillée sur sa chaise,
du cacao sur sa chemise, les pneus de sa mob dégonflés,
une fausse lettre d'amour écrite par la boulotte de la classe,
et en allemand j'ai arrêté de l'aider.
Pour moi il n'existait plus, j'étais furieuse, furieuse.

Quel malheur, juste devant le marchand de glace
mon argent était tombé dans les égouts.
Je pleurais à chaudes larmes.
À ce moment Helmut est sorti du magasin,
le garçon le plus grand et le plus beau de toute la rue,
il m'a tendu son cornet et m'a dit : « Tiens-le, mais n'y
touche pas. »
Il essaya de lever la plaque des égouts, sans succès.
Alors il m'a dit : « Tu sais quoi, on le mange ensemble. »

« Tu lèches une fois, je lèche une fois. »
Ce fut notre premier baiser, détourné.

Le temps pressait, et...
nous devions travailler toute la nuit,
pour terminer l'exposé pour le cours sur les contes de fées.
Elle tira la dernière feuille de la machine à écrire,
vint vers moi et m'embrassa.
Avec la langue. J'étais choqué.
Blanche-neige, avec la langue. Car pour moi elle était
Blanche-neige.
La relation n'a d'ailleurs rien donné.
Le semestre suivant j'ai choisi un autre cours.
L'Opéra de quat'sous.

C'était samedi soir, et j'avais un gros chagrin d'amour.
Mon ami m'avait quittée,
et je l'avais aussi quitté, et vous savez comment c'est.
Alors j'ai dit à ma sœur : « Viens, on va au *Turmhof*. »
Le *Turmhof*, à l'époque, c'était un lieu avec consommation
obligatoire
et des petites tables rondes. Nous avons pris place,
commandé une bouteille de vin, et comme c'est chez les femmes :
ma sœur a dit : « Je dois aller aux toilettes. »
Nous sommes sorties, revenues, et devant le portier,
se tenaient deux hommes qui nous ont dit, à nous, gamines :
« Vous voulez venir avec nous là-haut ? »
J'étais perplexe. À l'époque nous étions si réservées.
J'ai dit : « Comment osez-vous nous demander ça ? »
Nous avons attrapé nos manteaux, nous sommes sorties,
à sept heures et demie au *Turmhof*, et à huit heures déjà dehors.

Nous étions à une grande fête. Nous avons dansé toute la nuit,
jusqu'à ce que les pieds nous brûlent. Vers minuit, n'en
pouvant plus,

nous avons retiré nos chaussures et les avons jetées dans un coin.
Nous avons continué, et on a dansé sur toutes les musiques.
Au matin, alors que nous voulions rentrer, plus de chaussures.
Nous avons cherché, peine perdue.
Mon amie a dû clopiner sur ses bas pour rentrer.
La gaieté s'était envolée, l'amour aussi. Peut-être que c'était
mieux.

Une chose est sûre, je n'ai pas toujours été aussi vieux,
et dans mes jeunes années je voulais même partir
avec deux belles femmes, en vacances.
Et après ? Nous allons au parking,
arrivés là, plus d'auto, volée.
Nous sommes stupéfaits. La première pensée :
« Pas d'auto, pas de vacances, pas de mer, pas de plage... »

Nous étions environ cinquante à ce cours, dont seulement
sept filles.
J'étais ami avec la plus charmante.
Un soir, après un cours, nous traversions le pont sur l'Elbe,
en dessous le fleuve large et calme, au-dessus la lune,
claire et ronde.
Alors elle a commencé à parler du caractère
spirituel et magique de la lune,
de son influence sur la terre, les plantes, les animaux...
J'ai rétorqué qu'elle était éloignée de la terre
de tant de kilomètres, et qu'elle avait un certain poids.
Ce qui l'a un peu irritée.
Quand, plus tard, je lui ai jeté une boîte d'allumettes au visage
et que ma démythification de la lune faisait encore son effet,
notre amitié se refroidit.
En fait, nous étions trois chiens après un os, comme on dit.
L'un faisait ses exposés, le deuxième écrivait
de merveilleux poèmes, qu'elle lisait avec bienveillance,
et le dernier lui rapportait les bas nylon de Berlin-Ouest.

C'était moi. On peut voir ainsi,
jusqu'où le charme féminin peut conduire un homme.

*

Chéri.
Chéri.
Chéri.
Chéri.
Chéri !
Chéri !

Deuxième Partie

Tournez !
Tournez !
Tournez !
Tournez !

*

« Une première couvée de canards fait son apparition sur le
nouvel étang,
une quantité de joyeux petits colverts
Ils ont à peine vingt-quatre heures, ils nagent déjà à la
perfection,
et savent chercher leur nourriture.
La mère cane les surveille, elle les rassemble,
et, sur la rive, elle leur offre chaleur et protection.
Les sarcelles des tourbières vivent principalement à l'est de l'Elbe.
Elles ne sont que de passage dans les régions ouest.
Les deux couples sont lâchés. Avec succès.
En plein été, neuf cannetons sont nés.
Peut-être va-t-on pouvoir acclimater ici ce canard plongeur.
À la fin de l'été, d'autres espèces
sont passées ici : le fuligule milouin, par exemple,
ou sa femelle, la fuligule milouin.
Le canard siffleur.
Le fuligule morillon.
Le mâle est huppé et la femelle brun sombre.
Les petites sarcelles ont grandi.
La première année du nouvel étang tire à sa fin
De nombreuses espèces s'y sont plu et s'y sont multipliées. »

*

Je ne peux pas y croire.
Savez-vous combien de fois nous avons répété ce pas ?
Maintenant tout est faux. Ce n'est pas croyable !

Allez, dare-dare, un peu plus vite.

C'est bon pour la poubelle!

En plus ils me mettent dans cette robe sombre,
fermée jusqu'en haut. Je déteste ça!

J'aimerais un petit décolleté.

Je préférerais.

Edith! Edith! Où es-tu fourrée? J'ai une chose importante
à te dire.

Edith! Où es-tu? J'ai une chose importante à te dire.

Quarante-cinq...

En scène, mesdames et messieurs

Ah oui, les seniors. De février 2000 à décembre 2004, nous l'avons joué 69 fois. Le plus âgé des seniors, Alfred, a 75 ans. Beaucoup en ont 70. Edith est la seule qui ne veuille pas continuer. Cela dit, elle l'a dansé jusqu'à son 65ème anniversaire. Le reste de la troupe de *Kontakthof* a écrit une longue lettre à Pina : «Nous voulons continuer à danser pour toi!» Ils voulaient continuer à danser *Kontakthof* comme spectacle invité, en tournée. Qu'est-ce que ça pouvait bien vouloir dire pour moi? Ne me dites pas qu'il allait falloir refaire le même processus depuis le début, tout reprendre à zéro! Je parlai à Pina. Elle n'allait pas leur mettre des bâtons dans les roues, les priver de ce plaisir, me dit-elle. Je devais consulter le directeur et trouver une femme qui pourrait éventuellement faire l'affaire pour le rôle d'Edith. I must be mad. Car désormais ma tâche n'en était que plus difficile. Ma nouvelle candidate ne doit pas seulement apprendre et maîtriser le rôle principal, elle doit s'approprier et répéter le rôle avec tant de professionnalité que rien ne transparaisse sur la scène des cinq ans de pratique qui lui manquent.

Quand je repense à la première de *Kontakthof* ou que je me repasse de vieilles vidéos et que je compare les capacités des danseurs au début avec celles d'aujourd'hui, c'est le jour et la nuit. Comparé avec l'assurance, la précision, la perfection qu'ils ont aujourd'hui. Il faut dire qu'au bout de cinq ans, on n'est plus un profane. Chacun est maintenant son propre moi sur scène. Voulais-je de nouveau assumer cette responsabilité? Recréer une telle proximité avec quelqu'un d'autre? Est-ce bien ce que je voulais? Si j'avais dit non, ils n'auraient pas pu continuer. Finito, basta. Je ne peux pas faire ça aux seniors, ils sont aussi devenus mes amis, après tout. Je continue. Ce n'est pas à moi que devait tenir leur échec. Parfois, je me dis que sans les anciens, j'aurais complètement perdu le lien avec Pina. Car pour le Tanztheater, je ne fais presque plus rien.

*

Une semaine loin de la maison – toute seule. Ça pouvait me faire du bien. Etre seule est un luxe qui m'avait jusqu'à présent rarement été réservé. A Weimar, j'étais logée au ‹ Grand Hôtel Cour Russe ›. Le premier jour m'y attendait dans ma chambre une coupe pleine de pralines de qualité supérieure. Avec une voracité de sanglier, j'engloutissais toutes les pralines d'un coup. Mais alors, toutes! J'en avais besoin. Le lendemain, j'allais les remercier à la réception. «C'est pour les hôtes très spéciaux», me dit la femme au comptoir avec un grand sourire. Je rayonnais. Au petit-déjeuner, je m'empressais de poser la question à la ronde et en effet: personne d'autre n'en avait reçu, que moi. Youpi! Et oui, le chocolat, quand il arrive à point, peut faire pour une femme un joli petit miracle.
Ainsi va la vie, Margarita se déclara malade le jour même de la représentation, à 15 h 30. Et qui devait la remplacer au pied levé? Qui, donc, je vous le demande? Moi, évidemment. E oui, car pour le spectacle *Kontakthof*, je ne suis pas seulement, au côté de Beatrice, la meneuse de répétition, mais aussi la remplaçante pour toutes les femmes. Etant donné mon rôle dans les répétitions, mes capacités de remplaçante sont tout à fait captivantes. Il n'y a tout simplement personne d'autre qui puisse être aussi vite prête à monter sur scène que Jo. Car chez des seniors, qui ont depuis longtemps dépassé les 60 ans, c'est vite arrivé que l'un d'eux tombe malade. Mais annuler une représentation, ça serait vraiment le bouquet. Plutôt avaler encore un cachet anti-douleur et hop, tenir jusqu'au bout. Et me retrouver sur scène, moi la danseuse, au milieu de tous ces profanes,

de tous ces hommes et femmes aux cheveux gris – c'est vraiment une expérience unique. Mais, excusez-moi, je corrige : ils n'ont pas tous les cheveux gris. Certaines des femmes se teignent les cheveux, ou se font des mèches. Des corps imparfaits, des pieds tordus, de gros ventres, des cous fripés, des varices sur les jambes, des poches sous les yeux, petits, grands, gros, minces, certains encore beaux, d'autres plus très beaux, un peu pour tous les goûts, bref : des personnes âgées. Des épaules qui s'affaissent, de fausses dents.

Un jour, Alfred, lors de la répétition générale – je lui dis pendant la pause : «Alfred, si tu cours comme ça jusqu'au milieu de la scène pour te laisser tomber aussi brutalement, de toutes tes forces, sur les genoux, tu pourrais bien finir à l'hôpital – n'en fais pas trop.» Il s'est mis à rire et m'a répondu dans le plus pur dialecte de Wuppertal : «Pas besoin de me le dire, Jo, je l'ai déjà remarqué moi-même, quand mon dentier a failli me sortir de la bouche.»

Oh là là... Sa femme Ursula a porté pendant un certain temps une perruque grise sur scène. Elle avait perdu ses merveilleux cheveux gris, épais, ondulés, à la suite de sa chimiothérapie. Eh oui, c'est comme ça. Un des seniors porte depuis longtemps déjà un postiche, mais plutôt parce qu'il a perdu ses cheveux dans sa jeunesse. Ça fait très naturel. Inge avait souvent à travailler avec lui pendant les répétitions – «De la tendresse pour soi-même et pour son partenaire». Il faut dans ce cas aller caresser les cheveux du partenaire qui vous fait face. Elle est devenue rouge jusqu'aux oreilles, toute gênée en venant me trouver : «Jo, pourquoi tu ne m'as dit qu'il porte un postiche ?» On a dû pour un petit laps de temps renoncer à notre Inge. Elle est tombée malade, des problèmes cardiaques. Elle devait faire face à une grosse opération. Mais six mois plus tard, elle est revenue, rayonnante, en pleine santé. *Kontakthof* sans Inge ? Non merci.

En tournée, on a aussi fait les fêtes les plus folles. Imbattable. On a ri, dansé comme jamais, fait les fous jusqu'au matin. Quand je participais à ces fêtes, j'avais du mal à tenir comme eux – que ce soit la joie de la délivrance après le succès remporté par la représentation qu'on venait de donner, les longs applaudissements largement mérités, cette bouffée d'air frais à l'idée d'avoir à nouveau réussi une représentation à leur âge avancé. Le bonheur à l'état pur. Et là, chacun a le droit de danser comme il veut. Sans corrections et même s'ils ont mal aux pieds et que dès 11h du matin le lendemain il faudra probablement enchaîner de nouveau avec la séance de critiques, ou bien une matinée l'après-midi. Une fois, Thea, la plus âgée parmi les femmes, s'est livrée avec Anke à une danse tellement loufoque et tordante – une improvisation de danse expressive. Ça te laisse baba. A la Wigman. Les danseurs professionnels, à côté, n'ont aucune chance de faire le poids face à eux. Ah oui, les seniors, les *Kontakthöfleurs*. Cette joie de danser, de profiter du moment, de vivre.

Sinon, quand on était en tournée avec les seniors comme spectacle invité, on a eu la plupart du temps de très jolis hôtels. Sauf à Toulouse, en France. Des chambres minuscules, des couvertures tellement rêches qu'on avait l'impression de dormir avec un cadavre de chat. Comme la salle du petit-déjeuner était petite, on était assis serrés comme des sardines. Puis on nous a servi le pain. De la baguette, bien sûr. Toute fraîche, croquante, croustillante. Hmmm, un vrai délice. Je m'en faisais une joie, commençai à manger, en tartinant la baguette d'une bonne couche de beurre et de confiture. C'est Anke qui a commencé : « Je ne peux absolument pas manger ça, je vais monter dans ma chambre chercher le pain allemand que j'ai emporté dans mes bagages. » Thea trempait le sien dans le café, comme ça au moins, ça le rendait mou. Inge avait déjà laissé tombé, après que la baguette lui avait entaillé la gencive. C'était tellement croquant et croustillant ! On en hurlait de rire. En le coupant en petits morceaux et en le mangeant avec précaution, les seniors purent quand même savourer le petit-déjeuner français dans cet hôtel à Toulouse. Le sol était jonché de miettes.

Quand on est en tournée, on reçoit avant chaque représentation une lettre de Pina :

Mes très chers,
De New York à Gênes, je vous envoie mes pensées
les plus chaleureuses et de grosses bises.
Je vous souhaite une merveilleuse représentation.
Je suis de tout cœur avec vous.
Toï, toï, toï.
Je vous prends dans mes bras, avec amour.
Pina   le 18 novembre 2004

Et encore une autre :

Mes chers et beaux,
Pas loin de vous, à la Lichtburg, je serai bien fort
avec vous en pensée, quand vous allez aujourd'hui de
nouveau enthousiasmer et inspirer le public de Wuppertal
et vos nombreux amis d'ici. Profitez-en et prenez-y plein
de plaisir.
Vous êtes tellement super !
Toï, toï, toï.
Je vous embrasse et vous prends dans mes bras,
de tout cœur et avec amour.
Toujours vôtre,
Pina   le 17 février 2006

C'est quand même gentil de sa part. Pour chaque spectacle dans un autre théâtre, c'est presque toujours les mêmes mots. J'ai gardé 15 lettres de ce genre. On fait 26 copies de

la lettre la plus importante et qui veut en prend une, la con-
serve, la colle dans un album à côté des autres ou la met plus
tard à la poubelle. On nous envoie aussi des roses. Une
chacun. Moi aussi, j'en reçois une. Ah, Pina. Elle voudrait
tellement que tout le monde l'*aime*.

Je trouve ça dingue d'avoir la chance de leur donner des
cours, à eux qui sont pour ainsi dire les enfants de la guerre,
et ça 60 ou 65 ans plus tard. Je viens d'un pays lointain.
L'Australie. L'Australie n'a pas autant d'histoire que
l'Allemagne. Chacun de ces seniors est un être humain, avec
son propre parcours, son destin, sa psyché, son âme, son
état de santé. Beaucoup d'entre eux ont déjà subi de lourds
revers de santé et du sort : cancer du sein, problèmes cardiaques, angine de poitrine, cancer du ganglion lymphatique,
ostéoporose, douleurs aux hanches, cataracte, tinnite jusqu'à
devenir sourd d'une oreille, fausse-couche, enfant mort-né,
mort d'enfants, et tout ce qu'on peut imaginer : eh oui, des
personnes âgées, quoi. Mais les seniors à qui j'ai affaire
maintenant ne baissent pas les bras. «Prêts au combat pour
la vie, Jo», voilà ce qu'ils me disent.

Quand les seniors me racontent des histoires de la guerre,
je suis toute ouïe. Nuit après nuit dans la cave, toujours à la
recherche d'un abri, le frère jumeau mort à la guerre, le père
disparu, la mère morte. Des mots comme bombardements,
bunker, famine, tickets de rationnement, persécution des
juifs, Hitler, évacuation – tout qui brûlait autour de nous.
Je ne connais tout ça que par les films. Mais eux, ils connaissent ça en vrai. Des enfants de la guerre, quoi.

Ils n'ont pas cessé de m'apprendre des choses. Sur la vraie
vie. Sur les dépressions et les relations aussi. Sur l'amour,
qui va, qui vient. Je crois qu'ils peuvent mieux comprendre
ma vie. Parce que ce sont des personnes très normales.
Je veux dire, si j'avais à choisir entre la danse et ma famille,
la réponse ne fait aucun doute : c'est ma famille qui passe
avant tout. Mes enfants ne doivent pas souffrir ou être lésés,

juste parce que je travaille. Je prends tout sur moi, tant que j'en suis capable. Une vie à deux voies. Une vie de famille avec les pieds bien sur terre est tout ce qu'il y a de plus normal, ça n'a rien de glamour ! Plus je passe de temps avec les seniors ou d'autres personnes normales, plus la vie de danseuse et de théâtre me devient étrangère. De nos jours, tout le monde est de toutes façons un ou une artiste. Je supporte à peine encore d'entendre ce mot. ‹L'art de vivre› comme on dit – peut-être, ou peut-être pas. C'est l'être humain qui m'intéresse au premier chef.

Mais quand même, quoi de plus passionnant pour les *Kontakthöfleurs* que de pouvoir plonger dans le monde du théâtre… Sortir du train-train quotidien. Pour leur avoir donné la possibilité de réaliser leur rêve, ils gardent à Pina une reconnaissance éternelle. En fin de compte, un cadeau inimaginable. Un enrichissement sans pareil pour les *Kontakthöfleurs*.

La danse me manque. Pina aussi, parfois. Il m'arrive même de penser que Pina est devenue ‹étrangère aux autres›. Ça tient sans doute à la responsabilité énorme qu'elle doit assumer et à son refus de baisser les bras. Chacune de ses chorégraphies doit être comme un cauchemar pour elle. Rester à ce niveau. Chaque pièce comme une naissance. Et combien de pièces / d'enfants nous a-t-elle offerts depuis plus de 30 ans? Baptiser des spectacles de danse seulement de longs mois après la première. C'est toujours palpitant quand, avant une première, monsieur Matthias Schmiegelt fait son apparition devant le rideau, au début, pour faire son petit discours au public: «Mesdames et Messieurs, chères spectatrices et spectateurs, au nom de Pina Bausch, je vous prie de nous excuser. La pièce que vous allez voir ce soir est encore en gestation, ce qui veut dire que si vous revenez voir le spectacle demain, ou après-demain ou après-après-demain, il est fort possible que la pièce ne soit plus la même que celle que vous allez voir ce soir pour la première.

Un titre ne sera rendu public qu'un peu plus tard. Merci de votre compréhension ». La plupart du temps, ça fait rire le public de Wuppertal. Ils le connaissent bien, le petit discours de Monsieur le Directeur, parce que ça a souvent été le cas ces dernières années. Et ils sont très compréhensifs, parce que ça vaut la peine d'attendre et puis parce que Pina, c'est la Pina Bausch de Wuppertal. Article exportable de la ville de Wuppertal. Produit de marque de l'Allemagne. La chorégraphe la plus recherchée au monde. La lauréate de tous les lauréats de la danse.

*Jo Ann Endicott**

*Traduit de l'allemand par Marie-Pierre Harder.

Si je me concentrais sur mon bras,
c'est mon pied qui se retrouvait de travers

On était à deux doigts de le rater, *Kontakthof*. Ulla et moi étions attablés pour le petit-déjeuner lorsque nous entendîmes un reportage à la radio sur un nouveau projet de Pina Bausch : le spectacle *Kontakthof* pour femmes et hommes de 65 ans et plus. Nous en devînmes blêmes de déception. Voilà qu'on aurait pu avoir l'occasion de rencontrer Pina et sa troupe de danseurs, de jeter un œil derrière les coulisses, d'avoir un aperçu de tout ça. Justement dans ce théâtre de danse que nous fréquentions depuis des années et dont nous connaissions tous les spectacles.

Après nous être ressaisis, nous passâmes un coup de fil à Wuppertal, et là on nous dit qu'on pouvait venir le jour suivant. C'est emplis de respect et le cœur battant que nous franchîmes le seuil de la Lichtburg. Plus de cent autres personnes y attendaient déjà.

C'est Dominique Mercy qui dirigeait notre groupe. Quelle joie et quel honneur ! Mais la joie fut de courte durée. Les mouvements pour la première diagonale me semblaient très difficiles et j'étais au complet désespoir de ne même pas pouvoir distinguer correctement les figures au début de la deuxième partie. C'est là que Pina fit son apparition dans la salle. Nous retînmes tous notre souffle. « Eh bien, montrez-moi donc ce que vous avez répété ces derniers jours. » Ça me laissa tout pantois. Après à peine 50 minutes de répétition, c'étaient déjà les auditions et les autres avaient déjà deux jours d'entraînement derrière eux. Je fus mauvais là aussi dans les diagonales et plus je m'approchais de Pina, plus mes bras s'alourdissaient. Bon, me suis-je dit. Voilà, c'est tout. Tu as vu la Lichtburg de l'intérieur, tu as vu Pina de près. Ça fera de jolis souvenirs. Quand elle a choisi finalement le groupe dans lequel je figurais («Je vous prends tous»), je n'arrivais pas à le croire.

Et ce fut le début d'une époque où j'ai vécu et appris beaucoup de choses. A commencer par ce que je ne voulais pas du tout savoir: à quel point j'étais incapable de contrôler mon corps et mes mouvements. Les danseuses et danseurs qui nous entraînaient, Ed, Beatrice et Jo, nous montraient un mouvement, qui semblait facile et élégant. Mais j'eus tôt fait de constater que mes sens et mon cerveau n'avaient absolument pas appris à discerner correctement ce genre de mouvements. Et ensuite: reproduire.

Si je me concentrais sur mon bras, c'est mon pied qui se retrouvait de travers. Si je pensais à sourire, je faisais de faux mouvements. Et apparemment, la liaison des synapses dans mon cerveau ne fonctionnait pas de manière à me faire mémoriser ces mouvements. Je prenais peu à peu conscience du haut degré d'entraînement, de concentration et de spécialisation des danseuses et danseurs que nous avions vus et – à fort juste titre – admirés sur la scène. Et que ni moi ni les autres n'allions jamais pouvoir parvenir au niveau de ce que les pros nous montraient, de ça aussi j'en pris conscience. Pina avait dit que la première devait avoir lieu trois mois plus tard. Mais c'est un an et trois mois que cela nous a pris.

La deuxième chose que j'ai apprise, c'est que les paillettes et le glamour ne forment qu'une infime partie de la vie qu'on mène au Tanztheater. Répétitions dans la salle de ballet de l'opéra. Ça fait très distingué, n'est-ce pas. Mais la pièce était plutôt petite et délabrée. Que ce soit là qu'un spectacle comme le *Sacre* ait vu le jour. Incroyable! Même la ‹ Lichtburg › n'a rien de luxueux. Un vieux ciné où l'on a enlevé les chaises, apporté des bâches pour le ballet et des projecteurs. Et le tour est joué.

L'art, c'est beau, mais ça donne beaucoup de travail, disait Karl Valentin. Il avait bien raison. On a commencé par répéter deux fois par semaine, puis quatre fois et enfin, avant la première, tous les jours. Et bien sûr, encore et toujours la même chose : placements, déroulements, croisements, entrées en scène. Jusqu'à ce que ça devienne clair pour tout le monde que la précision et la discipline sont indispensables pour que ça marche. Et là, Beatrice était précise et inflexible. Il n'y a que le mouvement juste qui soit juste, elle n'en démordait pas. D'où une grosse crise, qui atteignit son apogée quand les seniors réclamèrent de Pina qu'elle modifie la pièce. Nous n'étions après tout que des amateurs, et vieux avec ça, on ne pouvait évidemment pas tout faire comme la compagnie, à commencer par ce déhanchement obscène. Beatrice se voyait face à des collaborateurs revendicatifs et restait sans voix. Je trouvais ces revendications étroites d'esprit. C'est bien *Kontakthof* que je voulais et pas une version pour pantouflards.

Est-ce que ça s'arrêtait là ? Jeter un œil sur les conditions de travail des danseurs professionnels ? Où étaient passés le plaisir, la joie, l'euphorie ? Il y en eut aussi. Il y en eut aussi, mais seulement une fois que le succès se profila.

Un jour, j'attendais pour les répétitions à la Lichtburg près de la porte, et soudain voilà qu'elle était là, Jo Ann Endicott. Je ne l'avais encore jamais vue, mais beaucoup lu sur elle et déjà mainte fois regretté de ne pas l'avoir vue ‹live› sur scène. ‹ Jo Ann Endicott ! › m'écriai-je avec stupéfaction. Jo apporta de la chaleur et de la douceur dans les répétitions. Ses coups de tête et sa spontanéité nous amusaient toujours. Quand elle corrigeait Edith et plus tard Christa, j'adorais regarder et en profitais toujours comme d'une petite représentation au milieu des répétitions. Et j'ai aussi peu à peu compris que c'était son rôle, le rôle qu'elle avait développé. L'exubérance de Jo, sa douceur, sa fragilité, sa force y étaient enveloppées.

« Comment c'est, alors, de travailler avec Pina Bausch ? » nous demandaient à chaque fois nos amis à Ulla, ma femme, et moi. Evidemment, nous n'en avions aucune idée, car elle n'est venue que très peu de fois, toujours très cordiale. Et à la répétition suivante, Beatrice arrivait avec un paquet de corrections, sous-entendu : « Pina a dit que... ». Ce que nous avons remarqué, c'est que Pina contrôle tout. Quand il a fallu remplacer un rôle, un jour, ce n'est pas à Beatrice et Jo, qui travaillaient avec nous quatre fois par semaine, que revint la décision. Il a fallu envoyer des photos par fax à New York et c'est Pina qui a tranché.

Bien que Pina ait été absente la plupart du temps, c'est quand même à elle que j'ai eu affaire pendant tout ce temps, c'est-à-dire à elle à travers sa pièce, *Kontakthof*. Au début, j'ai pensé que je connaissais la pièce. Après tout, Ulla et moi l'avions déjà vue plusieurs fois. Pour commencer, je me suis rendu compte que la pièce contenait beaucoup plus de scènes que ce dont je me souvenais. Puis à force de la répéter et regarder, j'ai pris peu à peu conscience de l'intelligence avec laquelle la pièce est construite. Les ensembles alternent avec des solos ou les apparitions des petites filles roses. Les scènes enjouées alternent avec les scènes tristes, les scènes réglées avec des scènes désordonnées. La musique est re-layée par la parole. Plus tard, j'ai remarqué que la musique vient tantôt souligner l'atmosphère, tantôt commenter de manière comique ce qui se passe sur la scène ou créer un contrepoint. Une langue passionnante. Et pour finir, j'ai compris avec quelle habileté Pina utilise la totalité de l'espace scénique. A chaque endroit, dans chaque coin, il se passe quelque chose. Des diagonales compactes, des blocs frontaux, des contre-mouvements de profil. Et avec ça, les figures individuelles, turbulentes ou paisibles. Des rangées de chaises, surgissant du carré de la scène, ne cessent de se promener vers l'avant, vers l'arrière, dans de nouvelles fonc-tions. Rien que la chaise ! Un rire se perd encore jusqu'au plus profond derrière la scène, au-delà de la rampe s'avance une petite fille rose. Plus j'en approfondissais ma connais-sance, plus je me sentais bien dans la pièce. Et parce que je la comprenais, je voulais aussi que nous la représentions avec précision et j'acceptais les reprises parfois pénibles lors des répétitions.

Je pris peur en lisant qu'une semaine avant notre première, la compagnie allait aussi donner une représentation de *Kontakthof*. Ils nous volent la vedette, ils vont nous tourner en ridicule – voilà ce que j'ai pensé. Les jeunes corps, élégants et entraînés, avec l'expérience de la scène, contre nous, les vieux, marqués par la vie. Les pros contre les bleus. En fait, ça ne s'est pas du tout passé comme ça, mais ça, on ne pouvait pas le savoir. Avant la première, Beatrice et Jo nous ont beaucoup aidés. Beatrice par des corrections sévères, Jo en nous montrant qu'elle croyait en nous. Même la compagnie, avec ses ‹ toï, toï, toï › et ses vœux nous a donné des forces. Et c'était un très beau moment lorsqu'après la représentation les pros sont venus chacun féliciter les seniors qui avaient tenu leurs rôles. C'est comme ça que j'ai eu le plaisir d'être étreint par les longs bras de Lutz Förster. Félicitations ! Et c'est la meilleure distribution que je puisse imaginer, me dit-il. J'étais fier, jusqu'à ce que je comprenne le lendemain ce qu'il avait voulu dire. Les débordements d'enthousiasme du public lors de la première restaient pour nous tous un mystère. Je me disais, c'est parce qu'il n'y a que des amis et des proches que la claque est si enthousiaste. Que certains danseurs de la compagnie aient dit qu'ils avaient été bouleversés au point de ne plus vouloir redanser le spectacle, ça non plus je n'y croyais pas. Mais l'enthousiasme ne faiblit pas. En tournée et même après six ans, en 2006, à Wuppertal. Ce n'est qu'après avoir dû quitter mon rôle, pour cause de maladie, qu'en allant voir le spectacle avec Ulla, je pus mesurer son effet.

Le désir de reprendre grandit avec le temps. Lorsqu'on nous a demandé si nous étions prêts à revenir, nous avons été ravis et finalement, nous avons repris. Les seniors nous ont facilité le retour. Nous avions gardé un bon contact avec Jo et Beatrice et ainsi ce fut comme un retour ‹ à la maison ›. C'était bien de voir qu'entre Beatrice et les seniors s'étaient créés des liens forts et amicaux. On s'appelait de temps à autre. Beaucoup sont allés voir les spectacles-solos de Beatrice. Le travail en commun et les succès avaient fait naître un sentiment de solidarité.

J'ai vraiment aimé les tournées. Pas pour les voyages, je ne suis pas un fan des voyages en groupe. Mais pour les différentes réactions du public. C'était passionnant de voir et d'entendre ce qui fait rire les Français, les Néerlandais ou les Italiens, ce qui les touche, la manière dont ils expriment leur joie. Il y a des nuances très intéressantes. Mais en fait, ce qui était très étonnant, c'est que la pièce ait été comprise et appréciée partout. Même les réactions après la représentation ou le jour suivant en ville allaient droit au cœur. Là, c'est les Italiens qui ont été particulièrement ouverts et chaleureux. A Udine, on a été applaudis une deuxième fois devant le théâtre après la représentation. Le lendemain matin, en ville, on a nous a serrés dans les bras, embrassés, photographiés, félicités.

Maintenant on approche de la fin. J'admire les seniors qui ont fait partie du spectacle pendant la totalité du temps. Ils ont bien sûr contribué à ce que *Kontakthof* soit représenté si longtemps. Je sais quel gros travail Beatrice et Jo ont accompli. J'ai été prof et je connais bien l'effort que ça représente de toujours revoir les mêmes erreurs et devoir les corriger. Je sais combien de force il en coûte de se battre contre le confort facile et l'insouciance. Jo a dû répéter son rôle pendant longtemps avec Edith. Puis elle a dû tout reprendre à zéro avec Christa pour que *Kontakthof* puisse continuer. Beatrice a dû se battre contre l'attitude des seniors: «On connaît déjà tout ça, on connaît déjà tout ça.» C'est comme ça que *Kontakthof* a pu rester vivant.

C'était une belle époque, très intéressante pour moi et Ulla. Pas la réalisation du rêve de toute une vie, pas la sortie du trou noir dans lequel on tombe après la mise à la retraite. Mais la grande chance d'avoir un aperçu sur le travail de théâtre professionnel et de me plonger dans l'œuvre de Pina Bausch. Une chance aussi d'avoir à cette occasion fait la connaissance de gens charmants. Et c'était un beau cadeau d'avoir pu vivre toute cette expérience avec Ulla.

Karlheinz Buchwald[*]

[*]*Traduit de l'allemand par Marie-Pierre Harder.*

Kontakthof

con signore e signori oltre « 65 » anni

Un pezzo di PINA BAUSCH

Testo italiano di Beatrice Libonati

Kontakthof (il cortile dei contatti) è un luogo in cui ci s'incontra per cercare un contatto.
Per mostrarsi, per rifiutarsi.
Con paure. Con aneliti,
delusioni. Disperazione.
Prime esperienze. Primi tentativi.
La tenerezza, e ciò che da essa può scaturire,
è stato un tema importante di questo lavoro.
Un altro è stato per esempio il circo.
Mostrare qualcosa di se stessi, dominarsi.

Kontakthof è stato rappresentato per la prima volta nel 1978 a Wuppertal.
In seguito in numerosi paesi.
Il mio desiderio di vedere questa pièce, questo tema,
anche con donne e uomini dotati di una grande esperienza di vita divenne, con il passare del tempo, sempre più impellente.
Così trovai il coraggio di affidare *Kontakthof* ad anziani di Wuppertal sopra i 65 anni.
Né attori né ballerini.
Semplici abitanti di Wuppertal.

Nel febbraio 2000 finalmente era pronto.

In un primo tempo il tutto doveva essere un evento da non ripetere.
Per questo motivo fu girato in fretta anche questo film.
Nessuno prevedeva che *Kontakthof con signora e signori oltre «65» anni* negli anni successivi avrebbe viaggiato in molti paesi d'Europa.

Pina Bausch

Dialoghi

Prima Parte

Buonasera, sono di Parigi!
Io sono di Amburgo e sono sposata.

*

Come sei bello!
Come sei forte!
Magnifico!

*

Sembra un rospo. – Sì, e quegli...
occhi da triglia. – E i capelli stopposi!
Ella di certo li sta perdendo.
Con quel vestito sembra un girino. – O una rana!
Sì, e questo naso a cavolfiore!
Un cavolfiore! – Esatto, e le orecchie...
Guarda, la tocca pure.

Uno, due, tre...

Gambe corte e grasso corpo...
E la sua femminilità aggressiva.
Chissà se era già così brutta da bambina?
Ma certo. Anche lei ha i capelli stopposi.

*

Sto sull'orlo del pianoforte e minaccio di buttarmi giù.
Ma prima di farlo grido...
a squarciagola, perché tutti mi sentano.
Poi striscio sotto il pianoforte
e sbircio

con aria di rimprovero
e faccio finta di volere stare da sola.
Ma in realtà vorrei che qualcuno venisse qui.
Poi prendo la mia sciarpa
e provo a strangolarmi
sperando che qualcuno venga
prima che io sia morta.

*

Jutta, andiamo a mangiare.
Oh sì, ne ho proprio voglia.
Offro io.
Che gentile! Dove andiamo?
Conosco un bel locale. – Che tipo di locale è?
È qui a Wuppertal? – È fuori città.
Un locale italiano.
Oh no! Non ho voglia di cucina italiana.
Ma sì! – Prendiamo una bella cosa saporita?
Zampetto di maiale con crauti e purè di patate.
Possiamo prendere anche qualcos'altro.
Ci sono i tortini con cipolla e pancetta?
Allora dobbiamo andare in centro.
Oh si, forse è meglio.
Magari prendiamo frittelle di patate. – Sì, con zucchero e
cannella!
Oppure l'omelette con il prosciutto cotto.
Cavolo verde con patate e lardo.
Che dolce prendiamo?
Riso dolce con amarene.
Gelato alla vaniglia con ciliege calde.
Oppure prendiamo i waffel! Che leccornie!
Sì, e anche un caffè, una bella tazza di caffè.

*

Ahi!

*

Dove sei?
In teatro?
Ci sono anch'io.
Ci vedremo nell'intervallo, nel foyer.
Verrai giù?
Per il vestito?
Ma che stupidaggine!
Osserverò tutti attentamente. Ti riconoscerò.
Ci sono delle ballerine in scena. Le vedi?
Cosa dici? Non devo piangere?
Dove sei adesso?

*

Ehi, Peter!
Ehi, Peter!
Mostrami quello che hai imparato.
Mostrami il passo con le anche che hai imparato.
Togliti la giacca, non vedo niente.
Questo non può essere il passo con le anche
che abbiamo provato tanto. Guarda.
A destra, in avanti, a sinistra, e ancora in avanti e a sinistra.
Girati di spalle! Vorrei vederlo da dietro.
Su la giacca.
Non è possibile!
Rigirati di fronte.
Guardami. Movimenti circolari larghi e sinuosi.
A sinistra, in avanti, a destra.
Oh Peter, non si fa così!
Fallo camminando in avanti.
Peter, non è così. Da quanto tempo…?
Che cosa facevi mentre provavamo?
Non imparerai mai. Ti servirà ancora un anno.
Andreas, musica!

*

Uno, due, tre.

*

Che bello!
Inge, lo proviamo vestiti di nero?
Oh sì, tutti in nero.
Pronti?
Andreas, musica!
Basta, basta! Non è poi così bello.

*

Head.
Cheek.
Chest.
Stomach.
Knee.

*

Lasciami, vattene!
Non sono arrabiata, voglio solo stare da sola.

Werner, che succede? Stai di nuovo male?

Non sono arrabiata, voglio solo stare da sola.

Non è una novità.
Non vali niente, non hai niente e non sai fare niente.

Ursula!
Ursula!

Oddio! Adesso sei morto?
Forse neanche questo. Vecchio pustoloso.
Tipico! Tutti stanno in piedi e tu sei steso a terra.
Non hai brio né temperamento, sei flemmatico.

E adesso che fa? Che puzza!
Oh, sta fumando.

Sei uno zero, semplicemente zero.
Puzzone e pedante.
Ha gli occhi piccoli.
Non gli serve vedere altro a parte le sue sigarette.
Chi ha gli occhi piccoli è tirchio.

Una vita al tuo fianco... Ma non hai nessuno fianco.
Uovo schiacciato. Mi annoi.

Sembra un grosso bebè, non trovi?
Sì, con quelle guanciotte cascanti! – Guarda le sue dita-salsiccia...

Non vali niente, sei senza nerbo!

Basta che compri i panini, ha già i salsicciotti.
Com'è suscettibile! Salta come una ballerina sulla sua sedia.
Guarda, se fuma una sigaretta dopo l'altra,
deve essere spesso solo.

Ah, la nostra brava ragazza torna alla carica!

Ha ancora del prezzemolo tra i denti.
Non sa cosa sia lo spazzolino.

Sei l'incarnazione dell'errore!

E nemmeno il sapone?
Col sapone si laverebbe i denti.

Oddio, come ho potuto stare con te!
Dovevo essere proprio cieca!

Prima mangia del rognone, poi del prezzemolo e poi non si lava.
Sì, stando a come puzza!
Deve avere mangiato una testa d'aglio intera.
E se puzza così non avrà nessun amico.
Ha mangiato anche erba cipollina. *Nouvelle cuisine!*
Chi puzza è solo, credimi.
Certo, si vede che è solo. E poi guarda i calzini!
Sono settimane che non li lava.
Adesso ci mostra anche i calzini!
Perché hanno un buon odore!
Probabilmente ne è anche fiero, te lo dico io.

Werner!

Non ce la faccio più. Jutta, io me ne vado.
È proprio terribile.

Werner?
Werner?

*

Ich lasse meinen Körper schwarz bepinseln, schwarz bepinseln
Und fahre zu den Fidschi-Inseln, zu den Fidschi-Inseln
Dort ist noch alles paradiesisch neu
Ach, wie ich mich freu, ach, wie ich mich freu
Ich trage nur ein Feigenblatt
Mit Muscheln, Muscheln, Muscheln
Und geh mit einer Fidschi-Puppe
Kuscheln, kuscheln, kuscheln
Aus Bambus richt ich mir 'ne Klitsche ein
Ich bin ein Fidschi, will ein Fidschi sein.

*

Dovevo avere dodici, tredici anni. Provavamo sempre
ad avvicinare le ragazze.

A scuola era difficile: le femmine da una parte e i maschi dall'altra.
Ma un giorno decisero che avremmo fatto una gita.
Dovevamo andare da un contadino in campagna, via dalla città.
E avevamo anche un compito: quello di cercare le dorifore.
A quei tempi le ragazze erano carine.
Portavano dei bei vestiti, belle camicette e gonne.
Ci stavamo sparpagliando nel campo di patate:
le ragazze erano davanti a noi, nessuno ci osservava...
Decidemmo: «Gli passiamo davanti!»
Ci siamo messi a correre ed ecco che successe:
una ragazza cadde nel campo, nel solco,
era a terra con le...

Improvvisamente si tolse la camicia, il suo busto era ricoperto di tatuaggi.
Non avevo mai visto niente di simile. Mi sono girata e sono scappata.

Avevo circa diciotto anni
e avevo conosciuto un uomo che aveva circa venti anni più di me.
Era l'uomo dei miei sogni: occhi scuri, capelli scuri.
Io purtroppo non ero la donna dei sogni suoi.
Mi diceva sempre: «Bambina mia, sei troppo giovane per me».

Non avevo ancora deciso:
vado da quella mora
con gli occhi marroni e la figura sexy a Barmen
o dalla biondina con gli occhi blu
e il sorriso simpatico a Vohwinkel?
Mi sono detto:
«Lascia decidere alla funicolare!»
Prendi la prima funicolare che arriva!
Ho comprato un mazzo di fiori
e ho preso la prima funicolare.

Dovevo mettermi quello colorato e scollato
o forse quello nero trasparente?
Mi sono guardata allo specchio e ho detto:
«Non posso crederci!» Eccolo lì,
quel foruncolo che mi veniva in fronte
ogni volta che avevo progetti particolari.
Dovevo coprirmi la fronte coi capelli,
anche se mia madre diceva sempre:
«Lascia stare, così non ti stanno bene.
Hai una bella fronte alta, sposta i capelli dal viso.»

Mi ha invitato al ballo di fine anno ed ero molto felice
di conoscerlo meglio, anche se era presto.
Abbiamo noleggiato una barca sul lago di Baldeney,
e andava tutto bene, finché non persi il remo.
Volevo riprenderlo e caddi anch'io in acqua.
Ma non sapevo nuotare e prima che lui se ne accorgesse
ero già in difficoltà. Ma lui era bagnino
e non fece tante storie: mi tirò fuori.

Avevo conosciuto una bella donna.
Ci incontrammo, ero molto speranzoso.
Ci avvicinammo,
si spogliò e io rimasi come fulminato.
Aveva tatuaggi di teste d'uomo su tutto il corpo.
C'era solo un posto libero. Uno shock! Devo aggiungere altro?

Tornavamo a casa la sera in questo vecchio palazzo enorme.
Era il palazzo delle poste con una scalinata.
C'erano molti piani c'era un interruttore a tempo
regolato al minimo, perché la posta vuole sempre risparmiare.
Riuscivamo a fare mezzo piano
e poi la luce si spegneva. Era bellissimo...

Stava scendendo le scale.

Mi scostai per farla passare,
lei fece lo stesso e ci scontrammo.
Per un attimo sentii i suoi seni sul mio corpo.
Allora avevo tredici anni. Fu la mia prima esperienza
erotica.
Doveva essere un segreto ma resistei solo giorni.
Poi un ragazzino mi offrì della cioccolata
e gliel'ho raccontato.

Pensai: «Speriamo che venga da me.»
Somigliava a Jean Marais e allora amavo Jean Marais.
Avevo visto tutti i suoi film e quando la coordinatrice
diede il via,
i ragazzi vennero verso di noi, e Jean Marais venne da me.
Ero felice. In seguito...

Conobbi il mio uomo ideale nella scuola di ballo.
Oh, era bellissimo e ballava fantasticamente.
Mi conquistò subito perché la danza era la mia passione.
Tutto andava bene
finché non dovemmo imparare un passo nuovo.
Allora cominciarono i problemi. E non ci crederete,
ma un giorno era così scocciato che mi lasciò
in mezzo alla sala da ballo e sparì.

Le notti più belle sono le stellate notti estive.
E quando poi torni a casa con la fidanzata
le fai vedere le stelle.
Le stelle più grandi
sono i baci belli, lunghi e gustosi.
Le costellazioni invece sono i bacetti piccoli
che si disseminano qua e là... e naturalmente...
...anche se la strada è lunga, si accorcia.
Si passa da una costellazione all'altra,
e di colpo sei a casa.

Aveva studiato qui in Germania e quando tornò
nella sua patria, a Istanbul, mi portò con sé
e mi presentò a tutta la famiglia.
Ogni volta diceva: «Ecco la mia piccola *sümüklü böcek*.»
«Questa è la mia piccola *karinca*.»
Guardo nel dizionario: «Cosa significano
sümüklü böcek e *karinca*?
Sümüklü böcek è la lumaca e *karinca* è la formica.
Immaginate un po' me, 1,78 m, certo con i tacchi...»
«Una formichina...»

Non è venuto a prendermi. Gliel'ho ritornata:
con una spugna bagnata sulla sedia,
gli ho sparso cacao sulla camicia,
gli ho scritto una finta lettera d'amore dallo bombolo della
scuola
e non l'ho più aiutato in tedesco.
Non volevo più saperne di lui. Ero furiosa!

Che sfortuna! La moneta cadde nello scolo
davanti alla gelateria.
Stavo lì a piangere come una fontana,
quando dalla gelateria uscì Helmut,
il ragazzo più alto e bello di tutta la zona.
Mi diede il suo cono gelato e disse: «Tienimelo, ma non
provarlo.»
Cercò di sollevare la grata dello scolo, ma non ci riuscì.
Allora mi disse: «Ci dividiamo il gelato.
Una volta lecchi tu e una volta io.»
È stato il mio primo bacio. Con una piccola deviazione.

Avevamo poco tempo...
Dovemmo studiare tutta la notte
per finire il lavoro del corso sulle fiabe.
Tirò fuori l'ultimo foglio dalla macchina da scrivere,

venne verso di me e mi baciò.
Con la lingua! Ero indignato.
Biancaneve con la lingua. Per me era Biancaneve.
Non ci siamo messi insieme.
Il semestre seguente mi iscrissi a un altro corso:
L'opera da tre soldi.

Era di nuovo sabato sera e avevo dei dispiaceri d'amore.
Il mio ragazzo mi aveva piantato
e io lui. Sapete com'è...
Ho convinto mia sorella: «Dai, andiamo al *Turmhof*.»
Il *Turmhof* era un locale chic con l'obbligo di consumazione
e con tavolini rotondi. Ci siamo sedute
e abbiamo ordinato il vino.
Mia sorella ha detto: «Vado in bagno.»
Mentre tornavamo, davanti all'entrata
ci aspettavano due signori. Ci hanno fermato, noi due ragazzine,
e hanno detto: «Venite di sopra con noi?»
Ero perplessa. Eravamo così timide!
Ho detto: «Come osate chiederci questo?»
Abbiamo preso i cappotti e siamo uscite.
Siamo arrivate alle 7.30, alle 8 eravamo già fuori.

Eravamo a una festa. Abbiamo ballato tutta la notte
e i piedi bruciavano. A mezzanotte ci facevano così male
che ci siamo tolti le scarpe.
E così abbiamo continuato a ballare.
All'alba volevamo tornare a casa ma le scarpe erano sparite.
Non le abbiamo trovate.
La mia ragazza è tornata a casa solo con le calze.
L'allegria era sparita e l'amore pure. Forse è meglio così.

Certo è che non sono stato sempre vecchio come ora.
Una volta volevo addirittura andare in vacanza con due
belle donne.

Siamo andati insieme al parcheggio,
e ci siamo accorti che la macchina era sparita. Rubata.
Siamo rimasti di stucco e il primo pensiero fu:
«Niente macchina, niente vacanza, niente mare, niente
spiaggia...»

Eravamo circa cinquanta nel corso, di cui però solo sette
ragazze.
Ero amico di quella più graziosa.
Una sera passammo sul ponte dell'Elba.
Il fiume era largo e calmo, sopra di noi la luna era chiara
e rotonda.
Quindi lei cominciò a parlare
della magia della luna
e del suo influsso sulla terra, sulle piante e sugli animali.
Io pensavo solo alla sua distanza dalla terra
in chilometri e che aveva un certo peso.
Ciò la confuse alquanto.
Poi le buttai una scatola di cerini in faccia
e il mio commento poco romantico sulla luna non le era piaciuto,
così la nostra amicizia si raffreddò.
Inoltre eravamo tutti e tre ai suoi piedi.
Uno le faceva i compiti in classe, il secondo le scriveva
poesie meravigliose, che ascoltava volentieri,
e il terzo le portava le calze di nylon da Berlino Ovest.
Il terzo ero io. Capite bene che effetto...
ha sugli uomini il fascino femminile.

Caro.
Caro.
Caro.
Caro.
Caro!
Caro!

Seconda Parte

Girare!
Girare!
Girare!
Girare!

*

«Gli ultimi arrivati nel nuovo stagno
sono un gruppetto vivace di piccole anatre selvatiche.
Hanno appena ventiquatro ore ma sanno già nuotare molto bene
e procurarsi il cibo da sole.
La mamma anatra le sorveglia, le tiene unite
e dà loro calore e protezione sulla spiaggia.
Le anatre di palude vivono prevalentemente a est dell'Elba.
Si trovano solo occasionalmente a ovest.
Sono state messe in acqua due coppie ed è stato subito un
successo.
In piena estate sono arrivati nove piccoli.
Forse quest'anatra subacquea riuscirà ad ambientarsi qui.
Alla fine dell'estate si sono aggiunte
altre specie di anatre migratorie,per esempio il moriglione,
con la sua femmina.
Il fischione.
La moretta
col ciuffo bianco e nero il maschio e col corpo marrone
scuro la femmina.
Le giovani morette tabaccate sono diventate grandi.
Sta per concludersi il primo anno di vita nel nuovo stagno
per le anatre.
Molte anatre si sono incontrate, molte si sono riprodotte.»

*

Non ci posso credere.
Sapete quante volte abbiamo provato questo passo?

E adesso è tutto sbagliato. Non è possibile!
Un po' più veloce, avanti!
Orribile!
E poi mi fanno mettere un vestito scuro
chiuso fino a su. Lo odio!
Preferirei una piccola scollatura.
Mi piacerebbe di più.
Edith! Edith, dove ti sei cacciata? Ti devo dire una cosa importante.
Edith, dove sei? Ti devo dire una cosa importante.

Quarantacinque...

Signore e signori, sul palco

Ah, gli *anziani*. Dal febbraio 2000 al dicembre 2004 ‹lo› abbiamo messo in scena 69 volte. Il più anziano, Alfred, ha 75 anni. Molti ne hanno 70. Edith è l'unica che non vuole continuare. Ha ballato comunque fino al suo 65° compleanno. Gli altri interpreti di *Kontakthof* hanno scritto a Pina una lunga lettera: «Vogliamo continuare a ballare per te!» Volevano continuare ad andare in tournée con *Kontakthof*. Cosa significava questo per me? Per favore, non lo stesso processo da capo, la stessa identica cosa. Ne parlai con Pina. Lei disse che non lo avrebbe impedito, non avrebbe tolto il divertimento a queste persone. Ne avrei dovuto parlare con il direttore e trovare una donna che eventualmente sostituisse Edith. I must be mad. Il mio compito era infatti a quel punto ancora più difficile. La mia nuova candidata non solo doveva imparare ed eseguire alla perfezione il ruolo da protagonista, ma doveva anche esercitarlo in modo così professionale da nascondere i cinque anni mancanti di pratica sul palcoscenico. Quando ripenso alla prima di *Kontakthof* o guardo i vecchi video, confrontando le capacità dei ballerini di allora con quelle di oggi, scopro una differenza enorme. Oggi danzano così sicuri di sé, in modo così preciso e senza errori. Appunto, dopo cinque anni non si è più dilettanti. Ognuno adesso esprime il proprio Io sul palcoscenico. Volevo prendermi di nuovo questa responsabilità? Volevo avvicinarmi così tanto ad una persona? Lo volevo veramente? Se avessi detto di no, non avrebbero potuto continuare. Sarebbe stata la fine. No, agli anziani non posso fare questo, nel frattempo sono diventati per me anche amici. Continuai. Non sarebbe finito tutto per colpa mia.

Talvolta penso che senza gli anziani avrei perso del tutto il contatto con Pina. Non faccio quasi più niente per il teatrodanza.

*

Una settimana lontana da casa, da sola. Mi potrebbe far bene. Essere da sola è un lusso che fino ad oggi mi sono permessa solo raramente.

A Weimar ho soggiornato nel ‹Grand Hotel Russischer Hof›. Il primo giorno, in camera, mi attendeva una coppa piena di cioccolatini di prima qualità. Con la voracità di un cinghiale, li mangiai tutti in una volta. Proprio tutti. Ne avevo bisogno. Il giorno seguente ringraziai alla reception: «Per ospiti speciali», mi disse sorridendo la signora dietro al banco. Il mio viso si fece raggiante. Durante la colazione chiesi conferma agli altri ed era proprio vero: nessun altro li aveva ricevuti, solo io. Opplà! Sì, al momento giusto, la cioccolata può generare piccoli e piacevoli miracoli in una donna. E siccome alla vita piace giocare, il giorno della rappresentazione alle 15:30 Margarita si mise in malattia. E chi doveva sostituirla? Chi? Io, naturalmente. Si, per la pièce *Kontakthof für Senioren* non solo dirigo insieme a Beatrice le prove, ma sono anche l'eventuale sostituta di ogni interprete femminile. In rapporto alla mia funzione di direttore delle prove, le mie attività come sostituta sono interessantissime. Non c'è nessuno pronto a salire sul palcoscenico più velocemente di Jo. Nel caso di anziani che hanno già da molto superato i sessant'anni, può accadere facilmente che qualcuno si ammali. Annullare una rappresentazione sarebbe l'ultima cosa da farsi. Piuttosto si ingoia un analgesico e via. È un'esperienza singolare stare sul palcoscenico nelle vesti di ballerina tra tanti non professionisti, tra tutti questi uomini e donne dai capelli grigi. No, scusate, mi correggo: non hanno tutti i capelli grigi. Alcune donne si tingono o si fanno le sfumature. Corpi non perfetti, piedi storti, pance grasse, colli rugosi, gambe rigate di vene, borse sotto gli occhi; piccoli, alti, grassi, magri, ancora belli, ormai non più molto belli, un miscuglio: sono appunto persone anziane. Spalle cadenti, denti posticci. Una volta, durante una prova generale, nella pausa dico ad Alfred: «Se corri così al centro del palcoscenico e cadi sulle ginocchia con questa foga, può essere che dopo ti ritrovi all'ospedale: non esagerare.» Lui iniziò a ridere e rispose nel più stretto dialetto di Wuppertal: «Non importa che tu me lo dica, Jo, me ne sono accorto subito nel momento in cui la dentiera mi è quasi uscita di bocca.»

Ohimè! Per molto tempo sua moglie Ursula ha indossato sul palcoscenico una parrucca grigia. I suoi bellissimi capelli grigi, ondulati e folti, li aveva persi durante la chemioterapia. Eh sì, è proprio così. Uno degli anziani porta già da molti anni un toupet, ma più che altro perché i capelli gli sono caduti quand'era giovane. Ha un aspetto molto naturale. Inge, durante le prove, ha avuto spesso a che fare con lui: «Tenerezza verso se stessi e verso il partner». In quella scena bisogna toccare i capelli del partner che sta di fronte. Lei arrossì e si imbarazzò, poi venne da me: «Jo, perché non me lo hai detto che ha i capelli finti?» Per un breve periodo abbiamo dovuto rinunciare a Inge. Si è ammalata di cuore. Aveva di fronte a sé una difficile operazione. Ma dopo sei mesi ritornò raggiante e in salute. *Kontakthof* senza Inge? No, grazie.

Durante le tournèe abbiamo festeggiato come matti. Feste insuperabili. Abbiamo riso così tanto, ballato e fatto gli stupidi fino a notte inoltrata. Durante queste feste a cui ho avuto la fortuna di partecipare, io non potevo reggere il confronto con gli anziani. Sarà stata la felicità di sentirsi come liberati per il successo della rappresentazione appena conclusa, i meritati applausi, il sospiro di sollievo per avercela fatta ancora una volta nonostante l'età. Felicità pura. E ognuno, a queste feste, poteva ballare come voleva. Senza correzioni e nonostante i piedi doloranti e il fatto che probabilmente, il giorno successivo, alle 11 ci fosse di nuovo la critica o il pomeriggio una matinée. Thea, la nostra ballerina più anziana, una volta insieme ad Anke ha dato vita ad una danza, una ‹danza espressionista› improvvisata così strana e buffa. Da restare a bocca aperta. Alla Wigman. Ballerini professionisti non avrebbero potuto fare meglio. Ah, gli anziani di *Kontakthof*. La gioia di danzare, la gioia di godersi il momento, di godersi la vita.

Durante le tournée avevamo di solito hotel bellissimi. Solo a Tolosa no. Camere minuscole e coperte ruvide che la mattina ti lasciavano la sensazione di aver dormito con un gatto morto. Siccome la sala per la colazione era piccola, sedevamo stretti l'uno accanto all'altro. I camerieri ci portarono il pane, naturalmente baguette. Fresca e croccante. Hmmm, deliziosa. Fui contenta ed iniziai a mangiare la baguette spalmata con uno spesso strato di burro e marmellata. Poi Anke cominciò: «Questa non la posso proprio mangiare, vado in camera a prendere il pane tedesco che mi sono portata dietro.» Thea inzuppò la sua nel caffè, almeno così si sarebbe ammorbidita. Inge invece aveva già rinunciato a mangiarla, dopo che le si era conficcata nelle gengive. Era così croccante! Piangevamo dal ridere. Solo spezzando il pane a pezzettini e mangiandolo con prudenza, in questo albergo di Tolosa, gli anziani si potevano godere la colazione alla francese. Tutto il pavimento era pieno di briciole.

Durante le tournée, prima di ogni rappresentazione, arriva una lettera di Pina:

Miei cari,
da New York a Genova vi invio tanti cari pensieri
e cordiali saluti. Vi auguro che la rappresentazione
sia fantastica. Con il mio cuore sono con voi.
Auguri di cuore. In bocca al lupo.
Vi abbraccio, con affetto
La vostra Pina   18/11/2004

E un'altra:

Miei cari e belli, non lontano da voi,
nella ‹Lichtburg›, sarò con voi e vi penserò intensamente,
quando oggi ispirerete ed entusiasmerete
ancora una volta il pubblico di Wuppertal e
i vostri numerosi amici.
Godetevi quest'esperienza e gioitene.
Siete fantastici.
In bocca al lupo.
Vi bacio e abbraccio di tutto cuore e con affetto.
Sempre la vostra Pina   17/02/2004

È gentile da parte sua. Per ogni spettacolo della tournée
quasi sempre le stesse parole. Ho conservato quindici lettere
del genere. Della lettera più importante se ne fanno ventisei
copie e chi vuole ne può prendere una, la conserva, la incolla
in un album insieme alle altre o più tardi la butta via. Arri-
vano anche le rose, una per ognuno. Anch'io ne ricevo una.
Ah, la nostra Pina. Vorrebbe tanto essere *amata* da tutti.
Trovo incredibile che mi sia data la possibilità di insegnare
loro a danzare, a loro che sono per così dire i figli della guerra,
sessanta o sessantacinque anni dopo. Io vengo da un paese
lontano, l'Australia. L'Australia non ha così tanta storia
come la Germania. Ognuno di questi anziani è una persona
con una propria biografia, un proprio destino, la propria
psiche, la propria anima e il proprio stato di salute. Molti
hanno alle loro spalle gravi problemi fisici e disgrazie:
cancro al seno, problemi cardiaci, angina pectoris, linfomi,
osteoporosi, dolori alle anche, cateratte, dall'acufene alla
sordità da un orecchio, aborti, parti con bambini nati morti,
figli morti, tutto il possibile, è chiaro, sono appunto persone
anziane. Ma gli anziani con cui ho adesso a che fare non si
danno per vinti. «Suvvia, Jo, tuffiamoci nella lotta per la
vita!» Questo mi dicono.

Quando mi raccontano qualcosa sulla guerra sono tutta orecchi. Notte dopo notte in cantina, dover fuggire, fratelli gemelli caduti in guerra, il padre sparito, la madre morta. Espressioni come bombardamento, bunker, morire di fame, tessere annonarie, persecuzione degli Ebrei, Hitler, evacuazione, intorno a noi era tutto in fiamme, io le conosco solo dai film. Loro le hanno vissute sul serio. Sono appunto figli della guerra.

Da loro imparo continuamente qualcosa. Cose sulla vita reale, ma anche su depressioni e relazioni di coppia. Sulle vicissitudini dell'amore. Penso che loro possano capire meglio la mia vita, perché sono persone comunissime. Voglio dire che se devo scegliere tra il teatrodanza e la mia famiglia, la risposta è chiara: la mia famiglia viene al primo posto. I miei figli non devono soffrire o essere trascurati solo perché io lavoro. Mi sacrifico in tutto finché posso. Una vita su due binari. Una vita familiare semplice è una cosa normalissima, non ha niente a che vedere con il glamour! Quanto più tempo trascorro con gli anziani o con persone normali, tanto più mi sento estranea alla mia vita da ballerina e al mondo del teatro. Tanto oggigiorno sono tutti artisti. Questa parola non la posso più sentire. ‹Artisti della vita›, forse, o forse no. Innanzitutto a me interessa la persona.

Tuttavia è sicuramente un'esperienza avvincente per gli anziani di *Kontakthof* immergersi adesso nel mondo del teatro e farne esperienza. Saranno per sempre grati a Pina per aver loro permesso, sei anni fa, di realizzare questo sogno. In fin dei conti è un regalo inimmaginabile. Per gli anziani del *Kontakthof* è un arricchimento senza pari.

La danza mi manca. Talvolta mi manca anche Pina. A volte penso perfino che Pina si sia alienata dalla gente. Probabilmente dipende dall'enorme responsabilità che ha e che non vuole abbandonare. Ognuna delle sue coreografie deve essere per lei un incubo. Dover mantenere questo livello.

Ogni pièce come un parto. E quante pièce/figli ci ha regalato in più di trent'anni? Tenere a battesimo serate di teatrodanza dopo mesi dalla prima. È sempre un'interessante esperienza quando, all'inizio di una prima, il signor Matthias Schmiegelt si presenta di fronte al sipario per tenere un breve discorso al pubblico. «Signore e signori, care spettatrici e spettatori, in nome di Pina Bausch Vi chiedo scusa. L'opera a cui assisterete stasera è ancora in fase di lavorazione. Questo significa che se domani o dopodomani o tra tre giorni verrete ancora ad assistere allo spettacolo, la pièce che vedrete potrebbe essere diversa da quella di stasera. Il titolo verrà comunicato in un secondo momento. Vi prego di essere comprensivi.» La maggior parte delle volte il pubblico di Wuppertal ride. Conoscono anche troppo bene questo discorso del signor direttore, perché una cosa simile è successa molto spesso negli ultimi anni. E sono molto comprensivi perché ne vale la pena e appunto perché si tratta di Pina Bausch di Wuppertal. Articolo da esportazione della città. Marchio di fabbrica per la Germania. La più ambita coreografa del mondo. La premiata tra i premiati della danza.

*Jo Ann Endicott**

---

*Tradotto dal tedesco da Luca Acuti.

Quando mi concentravo sul braccio, il piede era in posizione errata

Ce l'eravamo quasi perso, il *Kontakthof*. Mentre io e Ulla sedevamo a colazione, la radio trasmise un servizio su un nuovo progetto di Pina Bausch: *Kontakthof* für Senioren ab 65. Impallidimmo per la delusione. Avremmo potuto avere l'opportunità di conoscere Pina, le sue ballerine e i suoi ballerini, di dare uno sguardo dietro le quinte. E proprio del teatrodanza che da anni frequentavamo, di cui conoscevamo ogni opera.

Quando ci fummo ripresi, telefonammo a Wuppertal e ci dissero che saremmo potuti passare il giorno dopo. Con il batticuore e un timore reverenziale facemmo ingresso nella ‹Lichtburg›. C'erano già più di cento persone. Il nostro gruppo veniva diretto da Dominique Mercy. Che piacere e che onore! Tuttavia il piacere non durò a lungo. Io trovavo molto difficili i movimenti per la prima diagonale, ed ero disperato perché non riuscivo nemmeno a riconoscere le figure all'inizio della seconda parte.

Poi Pina fece ingresso in sala. Tutti trattennero il fiato. «Dunque, fatemi vedere cosa avete provato negli ultimi giorni». Mi venne a mancare il respiro. Dopo i miei 50 minuti di esercizio, subito il provino, mentre gli altri si esercitavano già da due giorni. E nella diagonale fui poi effettivamente una frana, inoltre più mi avvicinavo a Pina, più le mie braccia diventavano pesanti. Ok, mi dissi. È finita. Hai visto la Lichtburg dall'interno, sei stato vicino a Pina. Restano bei ricordi. Quando poi lei scelse il nostro gruppo («Li prendo tutti»), non riuscivo a crederci.

Quindi subentrò una fase in cui vissi e imparai molto. Al principio, soprattutto qualcosa che non avrei voluto affatto scoprire: quanto poco potevo muovere e controllare il mio corpo. I ballerini e le ballerine che ci allenavano, Ed, Beatrice e Jo, davano l'esempio con movimenti eleganti e leggeri. Notai ben presto che la mia percezione e il mio cervello non avevano mai neppure imparato a riconoscere esattamente simili movimenti. Figuriamoci poi a imitarli. Quando mi concentravo sul braccio, il piede era in posizione errata. Quando pensavo a sorridere, sbagliavo i movimenti. La struttura delle sinapsi nel mio cervello non era in grado di trattenere simili movimenti. Lentamente mi resi conto di come dovevano essere allenati, concentrati e altamente specializzati i ballerini e le ballerine che vedevamo e che – a ragione – ammiravamo sul palcoscenico, e anche del fatto che né io né tutti gli altri anziani avremmo mai potuto raggiungere quei livelli. Pina aveva detto che la prima sarebbe stata fra tre mesi. Alla fine si tenne dopo un anno e tre mesi.

La seconda cosa che imparai fu che fasti e sfarzi rappresentavano solo una minima parte della vita nel teatro-danza. Le prove nella sala del balletto dell'Opera. Suonava elegante ed esclusivo. La sala era tuttavia piuttosto piccola e cadente. E lì doveva essere stata concepita una pièce come il *Sacre*. Da non credere! Neppure la Lichtburg è una sede lussuosa. Un vecchio cinema, fuori le seggiole, dentro le luci e i tappeti per il balletto. Finito.

L'arte è bella, ma esige fatica, diceva Karl Valentin. Aveva ragione. All'inizio provavamo due volte alla settimana, poi quattro, e alla vigilia della prima tutti i giorni. Naturalmente sempre lo stesso: posizioni, percorsi, passaggi, entrate. Finché non fu chiaro a tutti che occorrono disciplina e precisione, altrimenti non funziona proprio niente. E in questo Beatrice era scrupolosa e inflessibile. Insisteva che solo il giusto era giusto. A causa di ciò vi fu una grave crisi, che culminò nella richiesta da parte degli anziani affinché Pina cambiasse l'opera. Eravamo in fin dei conti dilettanti e vecchi, non potevamo mica fare tutto come la compagnia, men che meno quell'osceno passo col movimento dei fianchi. Beatrice si trovò di fronte a collaboratori in rivolta e restò senza parole. Io consideravo pedanti quelle richieste. Volevo il *Kontakthof* e non in una versione per pantofolai. È tutto qui? Qualche aneddoto sulle condizioni di lavoro di ballerini professionisti? Che fine hanno fatto il divertimento, il piacere, l'euforia? Ci furono anche quelli, ma solo a partire dal momento in cui arrivò il successo.

Una volta aspettavo vicino alla porta della Lichtburg l'inizio delle prove, quando improvvisamente arrivò lei, Jo Ann Endicott. Fino ad allora non l'avevo mai vista, ma avevo letto molto su di lei, e avevo rimpianto spesso di non averla vista in scena. Jo portò calore e affetto nelle prove. Le trovate spontanee di Jo erano sempre divertenti. Quando impartiva delle correzioni a Edith e più tardi a Christa, io stavo volentieri a guardare, considerandolo un piccolo spettacolo all'interno delle prove. E mi resi anche lentamente conto che quella era stata la sua parte, concepita personalmente da lei. L'esuberanza di Jo, il suo calore e la sua vulnerabilità, la sua energia mi fecero a poco a poco immaginare il *Kontakthof* con ‹la Endicott›.

«Com'è lavorare con Pina Bausch?», chiedevano ogni tanto i nostri amici a me e a mia moglie Ulla. Naturalmente non lo sapevamo, perché Pina veniva di rado, sempre molto gentile. Poi alle prove successive Beatrice arrivava con un pacco di correzioni, secondo lo schema: Pina ha detto... Quello che abbiamo notato è che Pina controlla tutto. Allorché una volta fu necessario riassegnare una parte, a decidere non furono Jo o Beatrice, che lavoravano con noi quattro volte alla settimana. Si dovettero faxare delle foto a New York, e fu Pina a scegliere.

Sebbene lei per la maggior parte del tempo fosse assente, io mi confrontavo tutto il tempo con Pina, attraverso il *Kontakthof*. All'inizio pensavo di conoscere la pièce. Io e Ulla in definitiva l'avevamo già vista un paio di volte.

Dapprincipio notai che aveva molte più scene di quanto ricordassi. Poi, durante le prove e stando a guardare, mi resi lentamente conto di come la pièce fosse magistralmente composta. Compatte scene di gruppo si alternano a performance individuali o agli interventi delle ragazze rosa. Le scene gaie si alternano con altre tristi, quelle ordinate con le caotiche. La musica cede il posto al parlato. Più tardi riconobbi come talvolta la musica sottolinei l'atmosfera, altre volte la commenti ironicamente o faccia da contrappunto. Una cosa avvincente. Da ultimo compresi la sapienza con cui Pina utilizza l'intero spazio scenico. In ogni punto e in ogni angolo accade prima o poi qualcosa. Diagonali compatte, blocchi frontali, contromovimenti di profilo. In più singole figure agitate e altre quiete.

File di sedie dal quadrato scenico che si muovono in avanti o indietro con sempre nuove funzioni. L'uso della sedia! Una risata conduce fin dietro la scena, una ragazza rosa si spinge fuori dalla ribalta. Più arrivavo a comprendere, più a mio agio mi sentivo nella pièce. Siccome riuscivo a capirla, desideravo anche che ci attenessimo fedelmente alle indicazioni, e accettavo di buon grado le faticose ripetizioni nelle prove. Quando però lessi che a una settimana dalla nostra prima, anche la compagnia avrebbe rappresentato il *Kontakthof*, restai esterrefatto. Ci rubano la scena, ci vogliono mettere in ridicolo, furono i miei pensieri. I giovani corpi dei professionisti, eleganti e allenati, con la loro esperienza scenica contro noi vecchi segnati dalla vita. I professionisti contro i dilettanti. Andò in tutt'altro modo, ma non lo potevamo sapere. Alla vigilia della prima, Beatrice e Jo ci aiutarono molto. Beatrice con le sue severe correzioni, Jo mostrando di avere fiducia in noi. Anche la compagnia ci infuse coraggio con gli auguri e gli ‹in bocca al lupo›. Un gesto particolarmente bello avvenne quando, dopo la rappresentazione, i singoli professionisti si congratularono con gli anziani che avevano interpretato la rispettiva parte. Così io ebbi il piacere di essere avvinto dalle lunghe braccia di Lutz Förster. Complimenti, il miglior interprete che riesca a immaginare, mi disse. Ero orgoglioso, finché il giorno dopo non compresi cosa intendeva dire.

Noi tutti non riuscivamo a comprendere il giubilo del pubblico dopo la prima. Anche quando alcuni ballerini della compagnia affermarono di essere assolutamente commossi e di non voler più fare lo spettacolo, io non ci credetti. Ma il tripudio restò. Nelle tournée e anche sei anni più tardi, nel 2006 a Wuppertal. Solo dopo aver abbandonato per malattia, quando vidi lo spettacolo con Ulla, riuscii a comprenderne l'efficacia.

Il desiderio di riprendere crebbe nuovamente col passare del tempo. Fummo felici quando ci chiesero se non volessimo ricominciare e infine accettammo. Gli altri anziani agevolarono il nostro ritorno. Avevamo mantenuto un certo contatto con Jo e Beatrice, per cui fu come ‹tornare a casa›. Fu piacevole constatare che tra Beatrice e gli anziani si era stretto un legame forte e amichevole. Ci si telefonava di tanto in tanto. Molti andavano a vedere gli spettacoli da solista di Beatrice. Il lavoro comune e i successi avevano cementato un senso di complicità.

Le tournée me le sono godute. Non per i viaggi in sé, non sono affatto un amante dei viaggi di gruppo. Piuttosto per le reazioni del pubblico. Era eccitante vedere e sentire per cosa ridono i francesi, gli olandesi o gli italiani, che cosa li commuove e come esprimono le loro emozioni. Ci sono sfumature molto interessanti. Ma in verità fu davvero sorprendente che la pièce venisse compresa e apprezzata ovunque. Anche le reazioni dopo lo spettacolo e il giorno successivo in città furono molto toccanti. Gli italiani erano particolarmente aperti e calorosi. A Udine dopo la rappresentazione ci furono ancora applausi davanti al teatro. Il giorno dopo in città venimmo abbracciati e baciati, fotografati e congratulati.

Ormai anche quest'epoca volge al termine. Ammiro gli anziani che sono restati dall'inizio alla fine. È soprattutto grazie a loro che il nostro *Kontakthof* è stato portato in scena tanto a lungo. Mi rendo anche conto di quanto hanno dovuto lavorare Beatrice e Jo. Io stesso ho fatto l'insegnante e so quanta fatica costa vedere e correggere continuamente gli stessi errori. So quanta energia occorre per fronteggiare l'indolenza e la faciloneria. Jo dovette esercitare a lungo il suo ruolo con Edith. Poi dovette ricominciare daccapo con Christa affinché le rappresentazioni potessero continuare. Beatrice dovette affrontare una certa attitudine degli anziani: «Ma questo lo conosciamo già, ma questo lo sappiamo già». Così il *Kontakthof* restò vivo fino all'ultimo.

Per me e Ulla è stato un periodo bello e interessante. Non la realizzazione del sogno di tutta una vita, né l'antidoto al buco nero in cui si precipita con il pensionamento. Piuttosto una grossa fortuna. L'esperienza di partecipare all'attività teatrale professionale e l'opportunità di confrontarsi intensamente con l'opera di Pina Bausch. È stata una fortuna che nel contempo abbiamo potuto fare la conoscenza di persone così care. Ed è stato un dono che io abbia potuto condividere tutto questo con Ulla.

Karlheinz Buchwald[*]

*Tradotto dal tedesco da Luca Acuti.

When the Tanztheater tours to foreign countries, it is quite common that the words to the piece are performed in the language of the people. Here a paragraph to a performance in Taipeh. Of course tape recordings are necessary for learning. One very slow and articulated version and another fluently spoken.

Bei Tourneen des Tanztheaters in andere Länder ist es üblich, die Texte des Stücks in der jeweiligen Landessprache zu spielen. Hier eine Passage des Textes für eine Vorstellung in Taipeh. Natürlich gibt es zum Lernen dazu die notwendigen Tonbandaufnahmen, eine ganz langsam und deutlich, eine normal gesprochene Version.

Lors des tournées internationales du Tanztheater, il est d'usage de jouer les textes de la pièce dans la langue du pays d'accueil. Voici un passage du texte destiné à une représentation à Taipeh. Il faut naturellement pour apprendre le texte utiliser des enregistrements sonores, où le texte est dit tantôt lentement et distinctement, tantôt avec un débit normal.

Durante le tournée del Tanztheater in altri paesi è usuale che i testi della pièce siano recitati nella rispettiva lingua del posto. Qui di seguito un passaggio del testo per una rappresentazione a Taipei. Naturalmente, per imparare, sono a disposizione le necessarie registrazioni su nastro, con una versione del testo recitato con cadenza normale, molto lentamente e con pronuncia molto chiara.

KONTAKTHOF   TAIPEH

To Mr Urs Kaufmann   00 49 202 5638 171

我正站在鋼琴邊緣,而且我即將掉下去。
但在我做這個之前,我會大聲尖叫,
所以沒有任何人會錯過它。
然後我會爬到鋼琴下,憤世嫉俗地
往外看,假裝我要一個獨處,但實際上
我希望有人來。
接下來我會拿起圍巾企圖將自己勒死。
希望在我死掉前會有人來。

wǒ zhèng zhàn zài gāng chín biān yuán eǔr
chiě wǒ zhí jiāng didò shià chù.
Dàn zài wǒ zuò zèige zhi qián wǒ huè dà
shēn jiān jiào súo ì méi yǒ zhèn hé rén
huè zuò guò tā.
Rán hou wǒ huè pǎ dào gāng qín shià.
Fèn shì jí sú dì wàn wài kàn!
Jiǎ zuang wǒ yào ì gē rén dú zǔ.
Dàn shí jù shàn wǒ xī wǎng yǒ rén lái
aiè shià lái wǒ huè ná qǔ wěi jīn qù tú
jiǎng zěji lēi sǐ.
Shǔwǎng zài wǒ sǐ dià qián huè yǒ
rén lái.

Voila! It doesn't matter for the caramels
I ate some anyway this evening... I hope it
will have help you a lot. Many Kisses
Christel

Sometimes the text is purposely performed in a language
not meant to be understood.
For example this paragraph out of Kontakthof *remains in Russian*
when being performed in Germany, Italy and other countries.

Manchmal wird der Text aber auch in einer Sprache gesprochen,
die man möglichst nicht verstehen sollte.
Zum Beispiel diese Stelle aus Kontakthof *in Deutschland*
und Italien auf Russisch.

Mais il arrive parfois que le texte soit prononcé dans une langue
que l'on souhaite ne surtout pas voir comprise des spectateurs.
Par exemple, voici un passage de Kontakthof *en russe,*
destiné à des représentations en Allemagne et en Italie.

Talvolta il testo viene però recitato anche in una lingua che,
possibilmente, non dovrebbe essere capita.
Come, per esempio, nel caso di questo passo in russo tratto
da Kontakthof *rappresentato in Germania e in Italia.*

Guten Abend, sehr geehrte Damen und Herren.

Unser weltberühmtes Programm beginnt mit dem Auftritt unserer kleinsten Artistin, die aus dem sonnigen Italien kommt und als ~~letzter~~ *nächste* kommt in der Mitte unserer Bühne ein Mann mit einer sonderbaren Nase. Ja, meine Damen und Herren, diese Nase und diese Füße der Größe 47 sind auch für Euch etwas Bewundernswertes. Und dieser Mann: sein frischer Schritt und seine unwiderstehliche Eleganz – ganz einfach die Männlichkeit selbst.

Добрый вечер, уважаемые дамы и господа! Мы начинаем нашу всемирноизвестную программу с выступления самой маленькой артистки из солнечной Италии. Следом за ней на сцену выйдет мужчина с необыкновенным носом.

Да, уважаемые дамы и господа, этот нос, эти ноги сорок седьмого размера удивят даже вас. И этот мужчина: его лёгкий шаг и элегантность, перед которой невозможно устоять – просто само воплощение мужественности.

*Here an example taken from the notes and choreographic instructions
of a dancer's own role (Aida Vainieri).*

*Hier ein Beispiel der Notizen und choreografischen Anweisungen
einer Tänzerin (Aida Vainieri) für ihre eigene Rolle.*

*Voici une page de notes et indications chorégraphiques
d'une danseuse (Aida Vainieri) pour son propre rôle.*

*Qui di seguito un esempio di appunti e indicazioni coreografiche
di una ballerina (Aida Vainieri) per il proprio ruolo.*

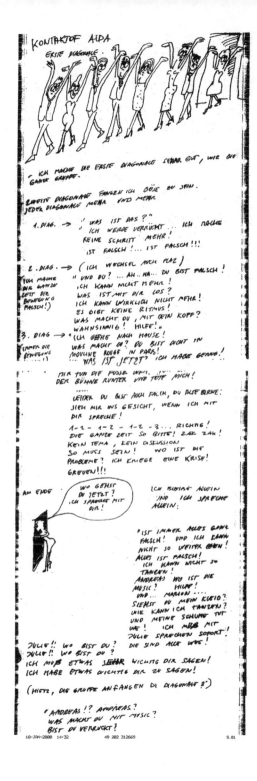

KONTAKTHOF AIDA

ERSTE DIAGONALE

" ICH MACHE DIE ERSTE DIAGONALE SEHR GUT, WIE DIE GANZE GRUPPE.

ZWEITE DIAGONALE FANGEN ICH BÖSE ZU SEIN.
JEDER DIAGONALE MEHR UND MEHR.

1. DIAG. →   " WAS IST DAS?"
" ICH WERDE VERRÜCKT... ICH MACHE KEINE SCHRITT MEHR!
IST FALSCH!... IST FALSCH!!!

2. DIAG. →   (ICH WECHSEL MICH PLATZ)
(ICH MACHE DIE GANZE ZEIT DIE BEWEGUNG FALSCH!)
" UND DU? ... AH..HA... DU BIST FALSCH!
ICH KANN NICHT MEHR!
WAS IST MIT DIR LOS?
ICH KANN WIRKLICH NICHT MEHR!
ES GIBT KEINE RITMUS!
WAS MACHT DU, MIT DEIN KOPF?
WAHNSINNIG! HILFE!"

3. DIAG →   (IMMER DIE BEWEGUNG...) "ICH GEHE NACH HAUSE!
WAS MACHT IHR? DU BIST NICHT IN MOULINE ROUGE IN PARIS!
... WAS IST JETZT? ICH MACHE GENUG!"

" MIR TUN DIE FÜSSE WEH!
DER BÜHNE RUNTER UND TÖTE MICH!

LEIDER DU BIST AUCH FALSCH, DU ALTE BIRNE!
SIEH MIR INS GESICHT, WENN ICH MIT DIR SPRECHE!

1-2 - 1-2 - 1-2 -3... RICHTIG!
DIE GANZE ZEIT SO BITTE! ZAK ZAK!
KEIN TEMA, KEIN DISKUSSION
SO MUSS SEIN! WO IST DIE PROBLEME? ICH KRIEGE EINE KRISE!
GREUEN!!!

AM ENDE   WO GEHST DU JETZT? ICH SPRUCHE MIT DIR!

ICH BLEIBE ALLEIN UND ICH SPRECHE ALLEIN:

" IST IMMER ALLES GANZ FALSCH! UND ICH KANN NICHT SO WEITER GEHEN!
ALLES IST FALSCH!
ICH KANN NICHT SO TANZEN!
ANDREAS! WO IST DIE MUSIC! HILFE!
UND... MARION....
SIEHST DU MEIN KLEID?
WIE KANN ICH TANZEN?
UND MEINE SCHUHE TUT WEH! ICH MUSS MIT JULIE SPRECHEN SOFORT!

JULIE!! WO BIST DU? DIE SIND ALLE WEG!
JULIE!! WO BIST DU?
ICH MUSS ETWAS SEHR WICHTIG DIR SAGEN!
ICH HABE ETWAS WICHTIG DIR ZU SAGEN!

(HIER, DIE GRUPPE ANFANGEN DI DIAGONALE 3.)

" ANDREAS!? ANDREAS?
WAS MACHT DU MIT MUSIC?
BIST DU VERRÜCKT?

Content / Inhalt / Table / Indice

Si vous désirez recevoir gratuitement notre catalogue
et être régulièrement informé de nos nouveautés,
n'hésitez pas à envoyer vos coordonnées à :

L'ARCHE *Éditeur*
86, rue Bonaparte
75006 Paris
commande@arche-editeur.com

ACHEVÉ D'IMPRIMER EN MAI 2007
SUR LES PRESSES DE L'IMPRIMERIE AGIT-DRUCK
À BERLIN
DÉPOT LÉGAL : MAI 2007

IMPRIMÉ EN ALLEMAGNE

Picture Format: 4:3 / NTSC / Color
Sound Format: Dolby Digital Stereo
Menu Language: English
Subtitles: English, French, German, Italien
Total Time: 149 min
Region Code: 0